EXPLORING SOUTH CAROLINA'S ISLANDS

Terrance Zepke

Pineapple Press, Inc.
Sarasota, Florida

Inquiries should be addressed to:

Pineapple Press, Inc.
P.O. Box 3889
Sarasota, Florida 34230
www.pineapplepress.com

Library of Congress Cataloging-in-Publication Data

Zepke, Terrance.
    Exploring South Carolina's islands / Terrance Zepke.
        p.   cm.
    Includes bibliographical references and index.
    ISBN 1-56164-259-2 (alk. paper)
        1. Islands—South Carolina. 2. South Carolina—Description and travel. 3. Atlantic Coast (S.C.)—Description and travel. 4. Islands—South Carolina—Guidebooks. 5. South Carolina—Guidebooks. 6. Atlantic Coast (S.C.)—Guidebooks. I. Title.

F277.A19 Z47 2002
917.57'09444—dc21

2002025339

First Edition
10 9 8 7 6 5 4 3 2 1

Design by Shé Sicks
Printed in the United States of America

Back cover photos all courtesy of Greater Beaufort Chamber of Commerce except second from top by Terrance Zepke. Front cover photos from top left clockwise courtesy of: Charleston Area Convention and Visitor's Bureau, Hilton Head Chamber of Commerce, South Carolina Department of Natural Resources, Terrance Zepke, Terrance Zepke, Hilton Head Chamber of Commerce.

CONTENTS

Acknowledgments

This book could not have been completed without the aid of many people who went out of their way to provide photographs, verify facts, and open doors to invaluable research. My deepest gratitude goes to a very special group of people, and I give my apologies to anyone I have overlooked.

Mike McKenzie, South Carolina Department of Natural Resources
Shawn Baldy, Dewees Island
Amy Ballenger and Ryan McCants, Charleston Convention & Visitor's Bureau
Melinda Kester, Edisto Chamber of Commerce
Bill Hall, Charleston Tea Plantation
Martha Kimbell and Duncan Wall, Greater Beaufort Chamber of Commerce
Debbie Stacener and Kelly Bonny, Hilton Head Island Chamber of Commerce
Sewee Visitor and Environmental Educational Center
Martin Coble
Georgetown Chamber of Commerce
Kiawah Island Visitor Center
Martha Heagany, Daufuskie Island
Georgetown County Library
George Wilson, Callawassie Island
John McKenzie and Jim Chaffin, Spring Island
Island Realty, Isle of Palms
Fripp Island Resort
Harbor Island Homeowners Association
South Carolina State Library
My family members (for riding, driving, navigating, and exploring all these places with me)
The gang at Pineapple Press

INTRODUCTION

I have long wanted to chronicle the islands of the Carolinas and reveal the offerings of each place, from historic homes to sunset dinner cruises. Researching and writing this reference was a labor of love. Can you imagine a tougher task than spending weeks exploring sea islands?

I must confess, I didn't realize how laborious the task would be! Multiple phone calls, e-mails, and introductory letters were necessary to obtain passes for access to the private islands. I was usually escorted by a representative from a resort or island development office. Calculating the duration of trips to smaller destinations was difficult. I often had to guess how long it would take to reach an island, fully tour it, ask my host all the necessary questions, take photographs, and arrive at another island in time for my next meeting. I was pretty good at this, if I do say so myself. My closest call was the day I made it to Daufuskie Island Resort's ferry terminal with less than nine minutes to spare. It was the last ferry of the day. If I had missed it and rescheduled, my itinerary for the next four days would have been blown. That's all I could think of as I stood on the dock waiting for my Dewees Island host. As the ferry was preparing to depart, my host jumped a barrier between the parking lot and the dock because it was the quickest way to the boat.

I've lived in the Carolinas for many years and have traveled the coast extensively while vacationing and researching my other books, *Lighthouses of the Carolinas, Ghosts of the Carolina Coasts,* and *Pirates of the Carolinas.* What a treat it was to rediscover some islands and to find others for the first time!

I wrote *Exploring South Carolina's Islands* for many different types of readers: vacationers, day-trippers, armchair travelers, and people looking to relocate to this area. I wanted this to be more than a good guidebook and hoped to convey the essence of each island through history, trivia, folklore, and specific tourist information. I divided the guidebook into three sections: Georgetown islands, Charleston islands, and Beaufort islands. Discussions of Georgetown, Charleston, and Beaufort are included, since anyone visiting area islands will want to see these wonderful port towns. In order to provide the most useful information, I have avoided listing specific fees and hours of operation unless there is a consistent policy. Nominal fees are noted with "$" instead of a dollar amount.

Most public and private islands of interest to tourists have been included. I excluded some places because they are completely inaccessible or are isles and not islands. Morgan Island, for example, accommodates more than 4,000 Rhesus monkeys and a research center. Pritchards is a 1,000-acre island leased by the University of South Carolina–Beaufort as part of its Center for Coastal Studies and sea turtle program. The 100-acre St. Phillips Island, owned by media mogul Ted Turner, is protected by a full-time caretaker. The 10.65-acre Moise Island is also privately owned and is used by the Moise family as a weekend retreat. There are several islands that are simply bedroom communities of Charleston and Beaufort, such as Distant, Dataw, Deer, and Polawana Islands.

During my research, I relied on many sources, including local and state tourism offices, local and state chambers of commerce, South Carolina State Archives, Library of Congress, local residents, developers, state government, and nonprofit agencies. Additionally, I used many excellent books to document island history, folklore, nature, and wildlife. (Most of these resources are listed in Additional Resources at the back of this book). I submitted every chapter to the above sources for an accuracy review. Please note, however, that hours of operation change seasonally, so it's always best to call ahead and confirm.

Some of the people I worked with voiced concern that tourists would try to enter restricted places or be disrespectful of nature and wildlife. Please, always watch for No Entry or No Trespassing signs; restrictions often extend beyond designated wildlife areas. Remember, never walk on sand dunes, pick sea oats, collect living sand dollars, feed or antagonize alligators, or disturb endangered loggerhead turtle nests or hatchlings. Be mindful that hurricane season runs June 1 through November 30 and that barrier islands are especially vulnerable to hurricanes. Furthermore, while all South Carolina beaches are open to the public, only residents and guests are allowed beyond the guard gates of private islands. Boaters can reach an island without trespassing, but are not allowed to use private boat docks or landings. A skiff or canoe can be brought onto the beach, forgoing the need for a dock, but visitors cannot proceed past the high tide point of a private island or they are trespassing.

South Carolina is home to some of the most engaging islands in the United States, and I hope you get a chance to appreciate them as much as I have. Take a leisurely carriage tour of scenic Beaufort or an eerie Charleston ghost walk. Spend the day beachcombing on Capers Island, or if you're looking for an indoor activity, visit the amazing Edisto Island Serpentarium. Play a round of golf on Cat Island's championship South Carolina National or partake in a cooking demonstration while staying in a cottage-style bed and breakfast on Knowles Island. Visit America's only tea plantation on Wadmalaw Island or simply sit down to high tea at

Georgetown's 1790 House. Take a pontoon boat ride out to Cape Romain Wildlife Refuge's Bull Island or go kayaking on the black-water Edisto River, complete with an overnight stay in a real tree house. Wherever you choose to visit and whatever you decide to do, I'm sure you'll enjoy exploring South Carolina's islands!

Author's note: Every effort has been taken to ensure that the information contained in this book is accurate. If you know of any revisions that should be made in a future reprinting, please send an e-mail to editorial@pineapplepress.com.

According to *Relax, Retire, Relocate in the South Carolina Lowcountry*, published by the Lowcountry & Resort Islands Tourism Commission, South Carolina has more than "200 sunny days every year, with April being the sunniest month."

MONTH	AVG. TEMP.	MAX. TEMP.	OCEAN TEMP.
January	49° F	59° F	52° F
February	52° F	61° F	54° F
March	57° F	67° F	59° F
April	66° F	76° F	67° F
May	72° F	82° F	75° F
June	77° F	86° F	82° F
July	80° F	89° F	84° F
August	80° F	89° F	84° F
September	76° F	84° F	80° F
October	67° F	77° F	73° F
November	58° F	69° F	63° F
December	58° F	61° F	54° F

I dedicate this book to my Aunt "Jack." Thanks for always believing in me and encouraging me in all my pursuits.

GEORGETOWN
ISLANDS

GEORGETOWN

Population: 15,889
Georgetown County population: 55,797

Georgetown, situated on the Atlantic Ocean where the Waccamaw, Black, Sampit, and Pee Dee rivers meet to form Winyah Bay, is the third oldest port in the state. It began as a Spanish settlement in 1526, but was later abandoned because of a "fever" epidemic. The English settled here in 1700, and the first land grant was issued in 1705 to John Perry by the Lords Proprietors. The first parish, Prince George, Winyah, was granted in 1722 to Baptist minister Elisha Screven and was recognized as an official port in 1729. It was five more years before this parish officially became Georgetown, so named after England's King George II.

Screven hired William Swinton to survey and divide 275 acres into lots. The preacher envisioned seven streets perpendicular to the Sampit River and five streets running parallel to it. Each block would contain 230 lots. Riverfront lots were one-quarter of an acre and all other lots were one-half of an acre. One hundred acres were put aside for a fort, school, prison, commons, courthouse, and Presbyterian, Anglican, and Baptist churches. At that time, everything shipped from Georgetown had to go through Charleston's port, where the customs office was located. Area residents pressured authorities to recognize Georgetown as an official port so planters and merchants could export directly without paying the steep freight charges for use of Charleston's port. Georgetown became an officially recognized port in 1732 and remained a very affluent community for many years.

The port city was heavily involved in the Revolutionary War and was

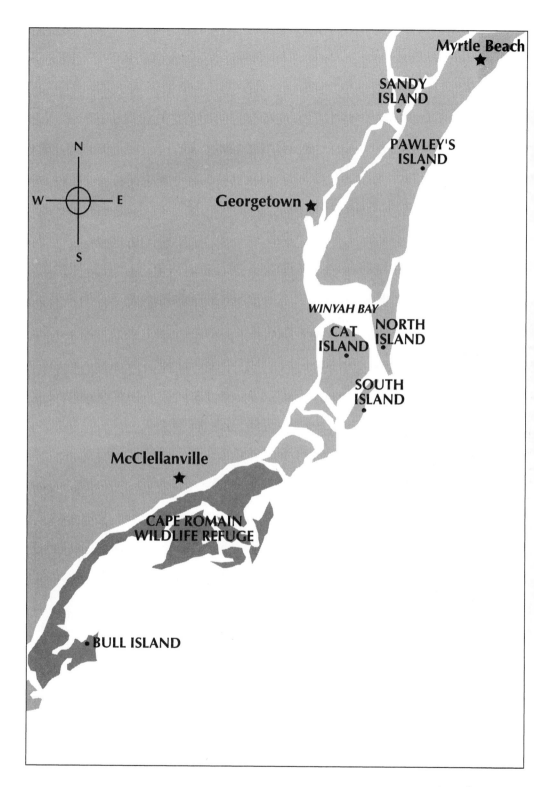

one of the few places in the state that was positively impacted by the war until Charleston was captured on May 12, 1780. Georgetown's very own Thomas Lynch, Jr., signed the Declaration of Independence. The Marquis de Lafayette, famous for his help in the battle against England, first arrived in America on nearby North Island on June 13, 1777. And, near the end of the war, the port supplied General Nathaniel Greene's army. For that reason, Francis "Swamp Fox" Marion led many rebellious aggressions around Georgetown. Marion received his nickname from the British because of his elusive tactics. After General Benjamin Lincoln surrendered to the British at Charleston, Captain Marion, an American colonist, gathered a group of men, hid in the swamps, and made bold raids against British troops, often defeating them. He was later appointed a brigadier general.

After the war, indigo plantations gave way to rice production. The Lowcountry, with all of its rivers, was perfect for growing rice. By 1840, Georgetown [County] produced one-half of all rice grown in the United States. In fact, it exported more rice than any other port in the world. Big, beautiful rice plantations lined what is now called the Intracoastal Waterway until the Civil War.

Union ships initiated a blockade on the port town in December 1861. Many planters fled the area, moving their families and slaves inland. By February 1865, both Charleston and Georgetown had been overtaken, slavery was officially abolished, and many former slaves raided abandoned plantations and took whatever they could carry. Many planters opted to move to Charleston rather than rebuild, and this deeply hurt Georgetown's post-war economy. Northerners came down and bought most of the old plantations at bargain prices. Prior to this, almost none of Georgetown's area plantations had been owned by anyone from the North; the buyouts must have been a hard thing for loyal southerners to witness. By the early 1930s, almost no native South Carolinians owned plantations in this area.

The Civil War was the beginning of the end of rice production in Georgetown. Descendants of slaves had no knowledge or interest in growing rice. Additionally, other southern states, such as Louisiana and Arkansas, began producing rice causing supply to become greater than demand. Several hurricanes in the late 1800s and early 1900s destroyed most of the remaining Georgetown crop. The economy was kept afloat by the new plantation owners, such as Archer Huntington and Jesse Metcalf, who hired local men to make improvements and staff the large homes.

Lumber production soon replaced rice. Georgetown had the biggest lumber yard on the East Coast and was prosperous again until the Depression. The International Paper Company set up operation in 1936, and by 1944 was the largest employer in the county. At the end of World War II, old plantations were sold to land developers who subdivided the land.

Georgetown's economy is again strong, thanks to commercial fishing, tourism, Georgetown Steel Mill, and International Paper Corporation. Today, the city's sixty-three homes and buildings in the historic waterfront district are laid out the way they were originally set forth by Screven, including street names. This scenic waterfront community has been rated among the top 100 small towns in America.

TOURS & ATTRACTIONS

The Historic District can be explored independently, or by taking a walking, trolley, or boat tour. Free maps can be obtained at the Visitor's Center. All tours depart from Front Street, either in front of the Rice Museum or the Visitor's Center (843-546-8437).

Arts Exchange, sponsored by Georgetown County Cultural Council, offers free programs and art shows. 10 A.M.-5 P.M., Monday-Saturday. 714 Front Street. (843) 527-2822. Free.

Dreamkeepers Center is run by the Committee for African-American Historical Observances. Tours featuring African-American homes, businesses, and institutions are offered daily. The center has art exhibits, artifacts, and historical photos and information. 10 A.M.-4 P.M., Monday-Friday. 1623 Gilbert Street. (843) 546-1974. Free.

Miss Nell's Tours provides walking and motor coach tours of historic Georgetown. Miss Nell is a native Georgetonian, former schoolteacher, and a member of the Georgetown County Historical Society. Tours depart from Harborwalk Books on Front Street. (843) 546-3975. $

Cap'n Rod's Lowcountry Plantation Tours offers three-hour plantation tours, evening harbor tours, shelling/lighthouse tours, and ghost cruises. Reservations recommended. Boarding takes place behind the Town Clock. (843) 477-0287 and capnrod1@aol.com. $

Cap'n Sandy's Tours also offers plantation river tours, evening harbor tours, and Lighthouse Island tours. (843) 527-4106. $

The Georgetown Tour Company offers a historic city tour, a ghost-busting tour, and an afternoon tea 'n tour. The tea and ghost tours require advance reservations and a minimum of twelve participants. (843) 546-6827. $

Kaminski House Museum was built in the 1760s by a wealthy merchant, Paul Trapier, as a gift for his daughter. The museum houses a large collection of fine antiques. Guided tours are offered on the hour. 10 A.M.-4 P.M., Monday-Saturday and 1 P.M. 4 P.M., Sundays. 1003 Front Street. (888) 233-0383 and (843) 546-7706. $

Front Street and "Big Ben"   Terrance Zepke

The Rice Museum, housed in the Old Market Building on Front Street and part of the Historic District, contains displays related to the rice plantation days. It is easy to spot because of the huge clock, which some refer to as Big Ben, mounted on the front of the building. (843) 546-7432 and www.ricemuseum.com. $

Swamp Fox Tours II provides tram tours of historic Georgetown. (843) 527-6469. $

ACTIVITIES

There are shops and a boardwalk along Front Street. There are also several antiques stores on Highmarket, Church, and Front Streets. A public boat ramp is located on Boulevard Street. For golfing information, see the Pawley's Island section or call the Georgetown Chamber of Commerce and request *The Tidelands of Georgetown,* a free publication detailing golf packages, area courses, and tee times. *The Tidelands* includes Pawley's Island, Litchfield Beach, Murrells Inlet, Andrews, Garden City, and Georgetown. (800) 777-7705.

Gul-R-Boy Charter Services specializes in red drum, flounder, spotted sea trout, tarpon, and shark fishing. Bottom fishing, casting, fly fishing, and sightseeing trips are also offered. Contact Cap'n Mike McDonald. 539

Harvest Moon Drive. (843) 546-3625, 520-6339, and www.gulrboy.com. $

The Jolly Rover Sailing Schooner takes visitors on two-hour pirate adventures. The crew, dressed as pirates, share local lore. Trips depart at 10 A.M. and 1 P.M., Monday-Saturday. Romantic sunset cruises around Winyah Bay are also offered. (800) 705-9063 and (843) 546-8822. $

ENTERTAINMENT & NIGHTLIFE

Nightlife is restricted to what area resorts, hotels, and restaurants provide. Myrtle Beach and Charleston are approximately an hour away in either direction and both have many jazz clubs, dance clubs, comedy clubs, and cigar bars.

ACCOMMODATIONS

Clarion Carolinian Inn is a beautiful inn overlooking the Intracoastal Waterway, just off Highway 17. It is next to the Hook, Line & Sinker Seafood Restaurant & Bar. 706 Church Street. (843) 546-5191 and (800) 722-4667.

Day's Inn is five blocks from the historic district and 9 miles from Pawley's Island beaches. (843) 546-8441 and (800) 329-7466. www.daysinn.com.

Econo Lodge is just four blocks from downtown Georgetown. 600 Church Street. (800) 55-ECONO, (843) 546-5111, (843) 546-8441, (800) 850-0078, and www.georgetown-sc.com/daysinn.

Hampton Inn is at Georgetown Landing Marina, right on the Intracoastal Waterway. 420 Marina Drive. (843) 545-5000, (800) 396-4122, and www.hampton-inn.com.

Jameson Inn is on Highway 17, next to Georgetown Landing Marina. (800) JAMESON, (800) 526-3766, (843) 546-6090, and www.jamesoninns.com.

Bed & Breakfast Inns

Alexandra's Inn is in Georgetown's historic district. All rooms have private baths and fireplaces. There is also a pool-side carriage house with whirlpool, two bedrooms, living room, dining room, full kitchen, and washer and dryer. 620 Prince Street. (843) 527-0233, (888) 557-0233, and www.alexandrasinn.com.

Harbor House Bed & Breakfast, circa 1765, is the only waterfront B & B in Georgetown's Historic District. It serves afternoon refreshments and all four bedrooms are equipped with private baths. Sitting rooms are on the first and second floors and a separate wet bar is provided. 15 Cannon Street. (877) 511-0101, (843) 546-6532, and www.harborhousebb.com.

1790 House Bed & Breakfast has six guest rooms and a cottage with private patio. The inn has a wraparound verandah, drawing room with fireplace, guest-use bicycles, complimentary evening refreshments, and more. Proper English afternoon tea is offered in their Angel's Touch Tea Room to guests and non-guests, but reservations are required. It has been recognized by Fodor's as one of the South's Best Bed & Breakfast Inns. 630 Highmarket Street. (800) 890-7432, (843) 546-4821, and www. 1790house.com.

The Shaw House overlooks Willowbank Marsh and contains a fully-stocked library, guest bicycles, private baths, and queen or king-size beds. 613 Cypress Court. (843) 546-9663.

RESTAURANTS

Most restaurants in Georgetown's Historic District are located on Front Street.

Front Street Deli offers subs, salads, soups, and desserts. Open 10 A.M.-4 P.M., Monday-Saturday. (843) 546-2008 and www.frontstreetdeli.dine.com.

Godfrey's Coffee Shop specializes in gourmet coffees and sandwiches, but they also serve quiche, salad, and seven kinds of bagels. (843) 527-3610.

Land's End is located at the Marina, as soon as you cross the bridge and enter Georgetown. Open for dinner and Sunday brunch. (843) 527-1376.

Pink Magnolia. This unpretentious, waterfront eatery has been written up by many publications over the years and has won several awards. You can't go wrong with anything you order, but my favorites are black-bean cakes, shrimp salad, and McClellanville crabcakes. Open lunch only. (843) 527-6506.

Orange Blossom Café offers soups, salads, sandwiches, burgers, and daily specials. Open for lunch and dinner Wednesday-Saturday, and lunch only on Monday and Tuesday. (843) 527-5060.

Rice Paddy Restaurant serves a lunch menu including soups, salads, pasta, and low country specials. Dinner includes fresh seafood, lamb, veal, and an extensive wine list. (843) 546-2021.

River Room serves McClellanville Lump Crab Cake (or crab ball appetizers), char-grilled grouper, soft-shell crab, pasta, chicken, steaks, shrimp, oysters, and scallops. It is famous for its shrimp and grits. Open for lunch and dinner, Monday-Saturday. (843) 527-4110 and www.TheRiverRoom.com.

Thomas Café, established in 1929, is a local favorite. They serve breakfast and lunch Monday–Saturday and brunch on Sunday. Brunch selections include blueberry pancakes, Cajun omelets, fried grits cake, and more. (843) 546-7776.

Fresh local shrimp, fish, crab, and scallops can be purchased at Independent Seafood Co.'s **Seafood Market** with free ice for shipping. Shrimp dock at 1 Cannon Street (on the waterfront in the historic district). Open 8 A.M.-6 P.M., Monday-Saturday. (843) 546-6642 and (843) 546-1122.

Conway's Cypress Inn also offers a full tea on the second and fourth Sundays of the month (two afternoon seatings). Finger sandwiches and baked goods are served on fine china and linen tablecloths. 16 Elm Street, Conway. (843) 248-8199 and www.acypressinn.com.

ANNUAL EVENTS

Annual Tour of Plantations and Colonial Town Houses (March) is a fifty-year-old tradition sponsored by the Prince George Episcopal Church. The majority of the plantations and homes are privately owned and are only accessible to the public during this three-day event. A different group of homes is on tour each day. Histories, maps, and a hostess to answer questions are available. (843) 546-4358. $

Harborwalk Festival (June).

Kaminski House Museum Gala (June) $.

A Celebration of Rice Festival (November) Gullah and plantation art and music are presented.

NEARBY POINTS OF INTEREST

Santee Coastal Reserve is 24,000 acres of the oldest wading bird rookery (300 species) still in use in North America. The reserve includes Murphy and Cedar, a couple of the larger barrier islands. Both are fairly wild with overgrowth, but there is a small beach and the islands are open to the public seasonally. The remains of rice planters' old hurricane towers can still be seen. Alligators, otters, beavers, deer, and bobcats also reside here. Primitive camping is allowed with a free permit from the reserve manager. Fishing is permitted in designated areas. There is a four-mile canoeing trail, which is accessible according to the season. Approximately three miles north of McClellanville on Highway 17 until turnoff to Santee Gun Club Road. For more information, contact the Department of Natural Resources or call (843) 546-8665. $

Bellefield Nature Center provides coastal environments, a saltwater touch tank, local wildlife, and research programs. Open year-round. Highway 17, south of Pawley's Island. (843) 546-4623. Free.

Hopsewee Plantation is a Georgian plantation house, circa 1740. It was the birthplace of Thomas Lynch, Jr., who signed the Declaration of Independence. A National Historic Landmark, this pre-Revolutionary War plantation has been owned by only five families. Open 10 A.M.-4 P.M., "by chance or by appointment," March-November. Visitors may tour the entire house and grounds or the grounds only for a reduced fee. Highway 17, 12 miles south of Georgetown and 48 miles north of Charleston. (843) 546-7891. $

Waccamaw River Heritage Preserve is 5,192-acres. Black bears and an array of birds inhabit the preserve, which is only accessible by boat. Restricted camping is permitted. (843) 734-3893. $

Belle Isle contains the remains of Civil War fortification, Battery White, which was built in 1862 to defend the entrance to Winyah Bay and the Santee River. Open daily. For more information contact Belle Isle Yacht Club. (843) 546-1423. Free.

Myrtle Beach State Park is 312 acres of nature trails, swimming, pier fishing, and crabbing. Wildlife includes songbirds, box turtles, lizards, snakes, loggerhead turtles (who nest during the summer), pelicans, bottle-nosed dolphins (seen offshore), and humpback whales (also seen off-shore). Bring binoculars for optimal viewing. Shower facilities, restrooms, nature center, picnic shelters, campsites and cabins, snack bar, and gift shop are available. Three miles south of Myrtle Beach on US 17 Business. (843) 238-5325. $

Outdoors Center Expeditions offers canoe and kayaking rentals and

Battery White was a Civil War fortification   Terrance Zepke

naturalist-guided tours on the Black River. Day and evening excursions are offered at all skill levels, including beginners. Sample tours: Black River Cypress-Tupelo Swamps, Chicora Wood Plantation and Sandy Island Nature Preserve, Huntington Beach Salt Marsh Creeks, and historic Georgetown Harbor (including around Goat Island). 21 Garden Avenue, Highway 701 North, 3 miles north of Georgetown. (843) 546-4840 and www.blackriveroutdoors.com. $

Huntington Beach State Park has 2,500 acres of salt marshes, freshwater ponds, maritime forest, and beaches. Ample bird-watching and alligator viewing is possible. Interpretive programs are offered daily. Don't miss a tour of Atalaya, which means "a tower overlooking the sea." The Moorish-style edifice was built as a winter home for Anna and Archer Huntington, who left the land and their former home to the state. Campsites are available. Three miles south of Murrells Inlet on Highway 17. (843) 237-4440 and www.southcarolinaparks.com. $

Across the highway from Huntington Beach State Park is **Brookgreen Gardens,** which was designed by Anna Huntington and is one of the most visited attractions along the Grand Strand. It contains over 9,000 acres of savannah, marshes, and beaches. Canopies of live oaks, formal gardens, sculpture gardens, and botanical gardens can all be enjoyed. Its wildlife park includes foxes, otters, and alligators. There is also a bird sanctuary and raptor aviary. A boardwalk winds around a half-acre swamp and there are picnic areas. Open year round. Located at US 17 South, Murrells Inlet. (843) 237-4218, (843) 235-6000, (843) 235-6001, (800) 849-1931, and www.brookgreen.org. $

Hobcaw Barony, a former plantation, is now a nature preserve and wildlife refuge, complete with visitor's center that contains fresh and saltwater fish tanks, displays, and audiovisual programs. Tours of the late Bernard Baruch's home, Belle Baruch's Bellefield and old plantations, stables, and slave homes, are given. Baruch was a Wall Street financier and presidential advisor who bought nearly 18,000 acres that encompassed ten rice plantations. Open 10 A.M.-5 P.M., Monday-Friday year-round and Saturdays seasonally. Eight miles south of Pawley's Island. (843) 546-4402, (843) 546-4623, and www.hobcawbarony.com. Free.

Hampton Plantation State Park has a three-mile walking trail, observation deck, and Hampton Plantation, which is reportedly haunted. Located between South Santee River and Francis Marion National Forest, 17 miles southwest of Georgetown, off US 17. From McClellanville, drive 7 miles north on US 17, and turn left onto Rutledge Road and follow the park signs. (843) 546-9361 and www.southcarolinaparks.com. Free.

Hudson's Flea Market is on US 17 Business, Surfside Beach. Open

Hampton Plantation is part of Hampton Plantation State Park, which is ten minutes from Georgetown. Terrance Zepke

year-round, but the hours change seasonally. (843) 238-0372. Free.

Murrells Inlet has several shops and restaurants. This fishing village is renowned for its Gulf Stream deep sea fishing and as the home of author Mickey Spillane. (843) 357-2007.

Myrtle Beach

In addition to the beach with its many restaurants and nighttime entertainment, there is an Amusement Pavilion, and Broadway at the Beach has a carousel, IMAX theater, Ripley's Aquarium, gift shops, and boutiques. Nightclubs can be found on Bourbon Street, along with many restaurants, such as Nascar Café, Joe's Crab Shack, and Hard Rock Café (Highway 17).

Off Highway 501, between Myrtle Beach and Conway, is the **Waccamaw Factory Outlet Stores**. (843) 236-5100 and (888) SHO-P333.

Queen Mary II departs from Waccatee Zoo and offers a one-hour scenic tour with narration, sunset cruise with entertainment, and dinner cruise. (800) 685-6601 and (843) 650-6600. $

River Rats offers **"Ratical" Guided River Trips** along the Pee Dee and Waccamaw Rivers in your very own electric pontoon boats. Guides accompany participants on all trips, which range from a half-day to two days. (877) 224-0700, (843) 650-1969, and www.river-rats.net. $

Carolina Safari Jeep Tours is open year-round and provides pick ups at most resorts. Learn about nature, history, plantations, ghost lore, and islands during the three-hour tour. There are great photo opportunities and wildlife viewing. (843) 497-5330. $

North Myrtle Beach

In addition to the beach, there are hundreds of restaurants, theaters, and shopping opportunities. Colonial Mall and Barefoot Landing are the biggest shopping facilities. Barefoot Landing has numerous boutiques, gift shops, outlet stores, and eateries, including House of Blues, Alligator Adventure, and Alabama Theatre.

A scenic boat tour is available aboard the *Barefoot Princess II*. Choose from a short sightseeing cruise, a lunch cruise, a sunset cruise with entertainment, a dinner cruise, and a dinner and show at Alabama Theatre. (800) 685-6601 and (843) 650-6600. $

Coastal Scuba has the largest custom dive boat on the strand and takes divers on half-day and all-day diving trips to see Carolina reefs and World War II and Civil War wrecks. Equipment rental available, including underwater cameras. (800) 249-9388 and www.coastalscuba.com. $

Debordieu Beach

South of Pawley's Island, just across the inlet, Debordieu has been called Yahany, Sandy Island, and later Dubourdieu, after Joseph Dubourdieu, a prominent early citizen of Craven County. The name has been spelled differently over the years, including Dubordie and Debidue, but is now known as Debordieu.

Joseph Alston and Theodosia Burr Alson (daughter of former US Vice-President Aaron Burr) spent summers here in their island home, "The Castle." On September 27, 1822, a massive hurricane claimed many lives and destroyed most of the property on Debordieu and North Islands.

During the Civil War, the blockade runner *The Dan* was nearly captured by Federals in 1864. The crew quickly made their way to Debordieu Beach and burned the ship and everything aboard so that nothing could be used by the enemy. They even succeeded in capturing some Union soldiers who followed them to the island.

Mrs. Robert Balding, who ultimately inherited Arcadia and Debordieu Beach, developed the area as a beach community complete with a golf course and a system of canals. Today, 1,250 homesites occupy 2,700 acres. Residents of this gated community enjoy 6 miles of beach, the Pete Dye Golf Course, tennis, and more. Vacation rentals are available. (800) 753-5597, www.debordieu.com and www.debordiwurentals.com.

TOURISM INFORMATION

Georgetown Chamber of Commerce. P.O. Drawer 1776, Georgetown, SC 29442. (800) 777-7705, (843) 546-8436, www.GeorgetownChamber.com, and www.GeorgetownSC.com.

Georgetown Visitor's Center is on Front Street next door to the Kaminski House Museum. (843) 546-8437.

DIRECTIONS & ACCESSIBILITY

Georgetown is conveniently located 45 miles south of Myrtle Beach (Highway 17 South) and 60 miles north of Charleston (Highway17 North).

∞ SANDY ISLAND

Population: 130-150

Named for the deep sand that surrounds this 12,000-acre island, Sandy Island was once home to nine wealthy rice plantations: Grove Hill, Hasell Hill, Holly Hill, Mt. Arean, Oak Hampton, Oak Lawn, Pipe Down, Ruinville, and Sandy Knowe. In 1927, Jesse Metcalf, nephew of Senator Jess Metcalf of Rhode Island, bought Georgetown area plantations Bates Hill, Glenmore, Holly Grove, Hasty Point, Breakwater, and Bell Rive. He later added Sandy Knowe, Oak Lawn, Pipe Down, Taylor Hill, Ruinville, and Oakhampton. He had a hunting lodge complete with stables and kennels for his polo ponies, hunting dogs, and bird dogs on his Hasty Point Plantation. He traveled between his many plantations in his speed boat, which was capable of 45 miles per hour. He sold these estates in 1936 because he refused to adhere to local Prohibition laws.

The island didn't have electricity or telephones until the late 1960s. The forty-eight-square-mile island now has thirty or so permanent families. Some are descendants of freed slaves who worked the rice plantations, and they still refer to areas of the island by those plantation names.

This is the dock and schoolboat used by Sandy Island Residents. Most residents keep a vehicle on the mainland and one on the island, using their motorboats to transport them back and forth. Terrance Zepke

Families live about a half-mile inland, on the east end of the island, in a loose cluster known as "The Village." The homes have tin roofs, bright shutters, and pretty conch shells to decorate the porches. Most families own two vehicles, one to use on the island's rudimentary dirt roads and one they keep on the mainland. Residents commute by a school boat and private boats to the mainland.

At high tide, it takes five minutes, via the Intracoastal Waterway and an old rice canal, to reach a small dock near Highway 17 and Brookgreen Gardens. At low tide, the boat ride is ten minutes and is a little trickier. Although a bridge would make life easier, many are opposed because it would encourage unwanted development. Sandy Island is the largest undeveloped freshwater island on the East Coast. Its bluffs protrude 40 feet above sea level, making them the highest elevations in Georgetown County. Sandy Island is full of dense woods, sandy trails, white sandy beaches, and marsh. The island is strictly residential, with a small church and slave cemetery.

T O U R S   &   A T T R A C T I O N S

Blackriver Outdoors offers canoe and kayaking rentals and naturalist-guided tours on the Black River. Day and evening excursions are offered at all skill levels, including beginners. Sample tours include Black

River Cypress-Tupelo swamps, Chicora Wood Plantation and Sandy Island Nature Preserve, Huntington Beach salt marsh creeks, historic Georgetown harbor (including around Goat Island). 21 Garden Avenue, Highway 701 North, 3 miles north of Georgetown. (843) 546-4840 and www.blackriveroutdoors.com.

NATURE & WILDLIFE

The Nature Conservancy manages a 9,164-acre **Sandy Island Preserve,** which excludes The Village and other private properties. It is open to the public, during daylight hours. At this time, there are no organized tours but independent exploration is permitted. Visitors are requested to avoid private property, including The Village. There is no public boat dock, but there is ample space to moor small watercraft. On the north side, there are some very distinguishable walking trails. It is forbidden to feed wildlife; hunt; pick flowers, mushrooms, shells, and rocks; camp; cookout; or ride bicycles, horses, or motorized vehicles. Trash must be disposed of properly. (843) 527-2557.

DIRECTIONS & ACCESSIBILITY

This island is accessible by private boat only. Take Highway 17 to Sandy Island Road at Brookgreen Gardens.

✍ PAWLEY'S ISLAND

Population: 200 (permanent)

This four-mile long and one-quarter mile wide island is on the Atlantic Ocean and part of Georgetown County. Pawley's Island forms the eastern tip of the Waccamaw Neck, which is a narrow peninsula covering Murrells Inlet to Winyah Bay, which lies between the Waccamaw River and the Atlantic Ocean. Residents describe their beach community as "elegantly shabby." Pawley's is one of the oldest beach resorts on the Eastern seaboard, first used as such in the 1700s. Pawley's Island was named after Percival Pawley who received a land grant in 1711 for

❦ ❦ ❦

Dream a Little, Believe a Lot

In life both are essential, and why not?
When one sees Pawley's or Litchfield
Dreams are fine, but believing is real.

Scenic beauty bordered by rivers and ocean
Enhanced by nature's magic potion
She unleashed all facets of her creativity
Causing lasting impressions on one's memory.

Pawley's and Litchfield, tree lined banks breast the Waccamaw,
Picturesque woodlands extend to a scenic creek shore
Here nature presents one with a stunning encore!

—George F. Brown Sr., Pawley's Island resident and local poet
(*as printed in* Pawley's Island/Litchfield Guide to Accommodations,
Activities, Dining, Services & Shopping)

❧ ❧ ❧

"Waccamau River to the sea [marsh]."

Places like Pawley's Island were used as an escape from the deadly "fever"—malaria. While no one at that time knew that the mosquito, which bred in the stagnant water of the flooded rice fields, was the cause of malaria, it was realized that the deadly disease had something to do with summer and plantations. Therefore, planters and their families left their homes every June and didn't return until November. Some wealthy families headed north or to the mountains, but most moved to area sea islands where they had second homes or were guests of family or friends. The danger was so well known that no visitor wanted to be stuck on a plantation on a hot, summer night.

Homes were built on brick foundations that extended high enough to prevent flooding, using the best timber and cypress. Outbuildings included kitchens, which were built outside the house for cooling purposes, servants' houses, stables, chicken houses, and outhouses. Ten of these original houses still exist today.

Passenger ferries used to be the primary way to transport residents and visitors across Winyah Bay and the Waccamaw River. The first ferry, Wasso Ferry, began operating in 1731 and delivered mail and freight. Even after steamboats came into service, it was still an all-day commute from Georgetown to Pawley's Island. Upon arrival on the island horse-drawn carriages and, later, cars carried supplies and families back home.

The All Saints Church was established in 1767 on land donated by George Pawley II. Slaves were taught the Bible and were baptized and made members of whatever church their master belonged to. By 1862, there were 289 slaves attending All Saints Church. Thirteen chapels were built for them on various plantations, and one still stands at Highway 17 and Old Shell Road that is used for special services and Sunday school.

All Saints Academy was established in 1838 for schooling the island's children. In the summer, children continued their studies, did chores, swam, and went horseback riding on the beach. The men belonged to the Hot and Hot Fish Club. They met every Friday afternoon from June through October at a clubhouse on the northern tip of the island. They played games, fished, cooked, and ate their catch. When the War Between the States ended, the freedmen demolished the old clubhouse.

President George Washington visited the island in 1791, and there was a skirmish here during the Civil War. There was a small battle on Pawley's south side in June 1864. Union troops tried to claim the blockade runner, *The Rose*, but a Confederate garrison prevented this from happening.

Salt was once produced on the island. The Indians were able to get salt from the ocean by evaporating the water and Percival Pawley learned how to do this, possibly from the Sampit or Waccamaw Indians. Records indicate he was selling and trading salt in 1782. According to *Pawley's Island...A Living Legend,* "The best description of the process was written in 1894 by William Hasell Wilson, in his 'Reminiscences.'"

> Shallow vats ten or twelve feet square, made of timber and elevated about three feet from the surface of the ground, were placed in pairs, each two being joined at the corners, two covers joined in a similar manner had a bolt, a junction which fitted into a hole at the junction of the vats. These covers could be swung around so as to be either over the vats or off. By means of a wind mill, salt water was pumped into the vats, and exposed to the action of the sun; when it rained the covers were swung around over the vats. After a certain time had elapsed, any water remaining was drawn off, and the salt which had been deposited allowed to get dry, and then taken to the storehouse.

Salt vats were active until 1863 when war ended production. This salt was used during the Revolutionary War by the Continental Army and during the Civil War by Confederates, until Union troops destroyed the equipment.

Some mammoth hurricanes have hit the island, including one in

Pawley's Island residents like their privacy, so it can be hard to spot many of the islander's homes. This is the Nesbit/Norburn House, circa 1842. Terrance Zepke

1893, Hurricane Hazel in 1954, and Hurricane Hugo in 1988. Remarkably, only a few houses have suffered any significant damage, which is a testament to how indestructible the cypress edifices are.

At one time, the Atlantic Coast Lumber Company owned several Pawley's Island dwellings for its employees. In 1902, the company built a railroad across Waccamaw Neck to the island. It was so badly damaged during a hurricane just four years later that the company decided not to reconstruct the railroad. By 1926, ferries and the road system had improved sufficiently so that the commute was much more pleasant and expedient. The Harold Siau Bridge (formerly Lafayette Bridge) was built in 1935, ending the need for ferries. A four-lane highway was finished in 1966, making the trip from Georgetown to Pawley's Island less than fifteen minutes.

Inns sprang up to accommodate visitors who discovered the pretty island. Among them were The Cassena, The Tavern, Tip Top, Sea View, The Pelican, and Newcastle. Some historic edifices that still exist today include Allston House, Casamar, Pawley House, Nesbit-Noburn House, Summer Academy, The Pelican Inn, Sandy Cot, LaBruce-Lemon House, Liberty Lodge, and All Saints Summer Parsonage.

In the 1920s, the island was known for its house parties, a tradition that continued into the 1930s and 40s. College students from all over the state and beyond flocked to Pawyley's during Easter break. The island is known for its excellent crabbing, shrimping, and fishing. Their sturgeon, including caviar from local sturgeon, and crab cakes are legendary. The town of Pawley's Island was incorporated in 1985.

TOURS & ATTRACTIONS

The small island is almost entirely residential. All shops, restaurants, and lodgings are on Highway 17, before the turn off to Pawley's Island. The historic homes of Pawley's Island include Joseph Blyth Allston House (Pawley House), R. F. W. Allston House, P. C. J. Weston House/Pelican Inn, All Saints Summer Parsonage/The Rectory, Ward House/Liberty Lodge, LaBruce/Lemon House, Nesbit-Norburn House, and All Saints Academy Summer House. All are located on Myrtle Avenue. In 1846, Governor Robert F. W. Allston built a causeway, known as Allston's Bank. In 1901, the Allstons sold their land, including the south causeway, to the Atlantic Coast Lumber Company for $5,000. It is the state's oldest causeway in continuous use.

Ask locals about the legendary Alice Flagg or read about her in my book, *Ghosts of the Carolina Coasts*. **Alice's Grave** is at All Saints Episcopal Church. Turn off Highway 17 on to Waverly Road. Go 2 miles to Kings River Road and take a right. The cemetery is on the left across from the church.

ACTIVITIES

There are no organized attractions, which is the appeal of this quiet island. Sunning, fishing (surf fishing yields flounder, whiting, and spottail bass), golfing, tennis, crabbing, sailing, reading, swimming, bird-watching, and beach combing are all favorite guest activities. Shelling is good seasonally.

Capt. Dick's Deep Sea Fishing offers sea bass fishing (a five-hour expedition), sundown fishing (an eight-hour expedition), and Gulf Stream fishing (an eleven-hour expedition for "really serious fishing, really deep water, really big fish"). Capt. Dick's also offers parasailing, jet ski and boat rentals, pirate adventure voyages, saltwater marsh and ocean sightseeing cruises. Murrells Inlet. (800) 344-FISH, (800) 344-3474, (843) 651-3676, and www.captdick.com. $

Walking and Bicycling **The Neck** is a popular pastime. It is only partially completed, but when finished will be a twenty-seven-mile scenic path extending from Murrells Inlet to Georgetown. Use of bike helmets is requested. (843) 237-4486, bike@chronon.com, and www.chronon.com/bike. $

GOLFING

Golfing is plentiful. In addition to the championship courses along Myrtle Beach's Grand Strand, there are some excellent courses in and around Pawley's Island.

Caledonia Golf & Fish has a restaurant and bar. Kings River Road, Pawley's Island. (843) 237-3675, (800)-483-6800, and www.fishclub.com. $

Heritage Golf Club. Heritage Drive, Pawley's Island. (800) 552-2660 and (843) 237-3424. $

Litchfield Country Club. Country Club Drive, Litchfield Beach. (843) 237-588 and (843) 237-3411. $

Pawley's Plantation Golf and Country Club has a Jack Nicklaus course. Highway 17, Pawley's Island. (800) 367-9959 and (843) 237-6009. $

River Club includes a course designed by Tom Jackson. Highway 17, Pawley's Island. (843) 237-8755. $

True Blue Golf has a Mike Stranz course and is a part of True Blue Golf & Racquet Resort. Kings River Road, Pawley's Island. (843) 235-0900, (888) 483-6800, and www.truebluegolf.com. $

Willbrook Plantation Golf Club has a Dan Maples Signature course. (843) 237-4900. $

BEACH AND SPORTS EQUIPMENT

Litchfield Beach & Golf Resort Recreation rents bicycles, racquetball equipment, a racquetball facility for a low hourly rate, baby buggies, and beach cruisers. (843) 235-5541. $

Pawley's Island Beach Service sells beach supplies and rents bikes, kayaks, umbrellas, and beach chairs. They claim to have the best prices around. (843) 237-4666, www.pawleysbeachservice.com, and www. islanderkayaks.com. $

The Golf Center offers rentals, repairs, PGA club fitting, trade-ins, special orders, and outdoor testing. (843) 237-1923, (877) 729-539, and golfctr@sccoast.net.

NATURE & WILDLIFE

Pawley's has a salt marsh, maritime forest, and beach. Wading birds can be spotted from the south causeway. These include great egrets, American egrets, snowy egrets, great blue herons, osprey, and white ibis. Other varieties of birds include ducks, brown pelicans, terns, gulls, and sandpipers. Loggerheads nest on the island in the spring, although these turtles nest here only every two to three years. Dolphins can sometimes be spotted from the beach.

ENTERTAINMENT & NIGHTLIFE

Nightlife is restricted to what the area resorts, restaurants, and motels offer, but there is still plenty entertainment available.

Mingo Moes in the Ramada Inn is a lively place that offers karaoke, shag, and beach music, as well as food and drinks. Litchfield Drive, South

One of the historical structures on Pawley's Island is P. C. J. Weston House/Pelican Inn. Terrance Zepke

Beach. (843) 235-0422.

Pawley's Island Tavern serves gourmet pizza, homemade barbecue, seafood platters, and more. Live entertainment nightly. Open daily 11 A.M.until . . . . Beside The Island Shops, Pawley's Island. (843) 237-8465.

Additionally, **Myrtle Beach** is only a half of an hour north on Highway 17.

ACCOMMODATIONS

True Blue Golf & Racquet Resort has luxury two- and three-bedroom villas overlooking its Golf Course. Amenities include outdoor pools and tennis courts. (843) 979-6123, (800) 449-4005, ctsleads@sccoast.net, and www.beach-vacation.com.

Hampton Inn Pawley's-Litchfield. (843)-235-2000, (800) 396-4122, and www.hampton-inn.com.

Holiday Inn Express has sixty-three rooms, each with one king or two queen beds. Each room has a microwave and a refrigerator. Deluxe continental breakfast is included. (843) 235-0808, (800) 830-0135, and hipawisld@aol.com.

Litchfield Beach & Golf Resort is the area's only oceanfront resort with three on-site golf courses, an award-winning tennis club, indoor and outdoor pools, health club, three restaurants, and meeting facilities. Guests stay in its hotel, condominiums, or villas. (843) 237-3000, (800)

845-1897, info@litchfieldbeach.com, and www.litchfieldbeach.com.

Litchfield Plantation Country Inn Resort has thirty-eight rooms and suites. The picturesque inn is at the end of a quarter-mile avenue of live oaks, on the site of a 1750s rice plantation. Gourmet dining is available in their Carriage House Club. (843) 237-9121, (800) 869-1410, vacation@litchfieldplantation.com, and www.litchfieldplantation.com.

Oceanfront Litchfield Inn offers lodge and poolside rooms, ocean-front efficiencies, two-bedroom villas, oceanfront bar and restaurant, and pools for adults and children. (843) 237-4211, (800) 637-4211, info@litchfieldinn.com, and www.litchfieldinn.com.

Pawley's Pier Village, Inc. is an oceanfront resort, complete with fifty-four fully furnished two- and three-bedroom condos, kitchen, washers and dryers, and private balconies overlooking the pool and a private pier. (843) 237-4220.

Pawley's Plantation Golf & Country Club has deluxe golf villas, a Jack Nicklaus signature course, an elegant clubhouse, restaurants, a Pro Shop, a golf school, tennis courts, a new conference center, and a ball-room. (843) 237-6100, (800) 367-9959, info@pawleysplantation.com, and www.pawleysplantation.com.

Ramada Inn is on the grounds of the Sea Gull Golf Club. Highway 17, Pawley's Island. (843) 237-4261 and www.ramadapawleys.com.

BED & BREAKFAST INNS

There are three historic oceanfront inns on Pawley's Island.

The Cassandra Inn. Atlantic Avenue. (843) 237-3760.

All twenty guest rooms at the **Sea View Inn** come with a private half bath, a large overhead fan, and a single and double bed or two double beds. Three tiled showers are available in the main house, and there are hot water beach showers for those returning from a dip in the ocean. A cottage behind the Inn has six rooms, some with a porch and all with air conditioning, cross ventilation from a central courtyard, and a fabulous view of the pristine marshes. The quaint inn is known for its excellent seafood and low country cuisine. Sample dishes include deviled crab, oyster pie, shrimp gumbo, jambalaya, and spoon bread. Each year Sea View Inn sponsors a wellness week, watercolor artist week, and a week for nature lovers. The inn, which has a large deck that overlooks the beach and ocean, is at 414 Myrtle Avenue. (843) 237-4253.

The Pelican Inn was built in 1858 for Plowden Weston, Lt. Governor of South Carolina. 506 Myrtle Avenue. (843) 237-2298.

VACATION RENTALS

The Dieter Company Real Estate Sales & Rentals has properties on Pawley's Island and Litchfield Beach. Highway 17, Litchfield Beach. (843)

237-2813, (800) 950-6232, and www.dietercompany.com.

The Lachiocotte Company is a full service real estate company, including vacation rentals for Pawley's Island, Litchfield Beach, and Debordieu. Lachicotte's Corner, Pawley's Island. (800) 422-4777, (843) 237-2094, and www.lachicotte.com.

Litchfield Real Estate offers rentals and interval ownership for Pawley's Island and Litchfield. Highway 17, Pawley's Island. (800) 437-4241, (843) 237-4241, and www.litchfieldrealestate.com.

Pawley's Island Realty Company says it is the area's largest vacation rental company. North Causeway, Pawley's Island. (800) 937-7352, (843) 237-4257, and www.pawleysislandvacations.com.

James W. Smith Real Estate Company has vacation rentals for Pawley's Island and Litchfield. Highway 17, Litchfield Beach. (800) 476-5651, (843) 237-4246, and jwsre@sccoast.net.

RESTAURANTS
Pawley's Island

Austin's Restaurant & Bar features contemporary American cuisine and many fresh seafood dishes. Austin's has great ambience and food from Chef Bill, a graduate of the Culinary Institute of America. Highway 17, Pawley's Island. (843) 235-3800.

Croissants Pawley's is a bakery that serves brunch, lunch, and dinner. They have a wonderful menu and delectable desserts, including specialty cakes available by the slice or whole. 10185 Ocean Highway, Pawley's Island. (843) 235-3000.

Craving a good hot dog or banana split? **The Dog & Cone** is on Highway 17, The Hammock Shops, Pawley's Island. (843) 237-0339.

Frank's Restaurant and Frank's Outback Restaurant & Bar offers fine dining and an extensive wine list. The menu changes nightly. Selections include Southwestern, French, Asian, Thai, chicken, veal, duck, lamb, and seafood. Lunch and dinner, Monday–Saturday. Highway 17, Pawley's Island. The Outback Restaurant is behind Frank's Restaurant. (843) 237-3030 and www.franksandoutback.com.

The Hook Restaurant & Bar's menu ranges from crab fritter appetizers to filet mignon. 10707 Ocean Highway. (843) 235-8656.

Pawley's Island Pastries is a bakery and coffeehouse in Pawley's Island Plaza. Specialties include apple fritters, brioche, cheese biscuits, peanut butter torte, and death by chocolate. If you're still hungry, they also serve sandwiches, quiche, and soups. Open Monday-Saturday. (843) 237-7242.

Magnolia Café has an extensive menu, featuring pizza, soups, salads, seafood, pasta, and steaks. Pawley's Town Square. (843) 235-2528.

The Purple Onion Café offers "lots of healthy goods, a dash of gourmets, and a sprinkle of Southern." 9428 Ocean Highway, Pawley's Island. (843) 237-8366.

Tyler's Cove features Cajun-fried chicken, teriyaki marinated tuna, black angus prime rib, and pork tenderloin. Highway 17, Hammock Shops, Pawley's Island. (843) 237-4848.

Roz's Rice Mill Café serves soups, salads, and sandwiches. Highway 17, Hammock Shops, Pawley's Island. (843) 235-0196.

Murrells Inlet
All of these restaurants are located on Highway 17 Business.
Nance's. (843) 651-2696.
Admiral's Flagship. (843) 651-3016.
Anchor Inn Restaurant. (843) 651-2295.
Bovine's. (843) 651-2888.
The Captain's Restaurant. (843) 651-2416.
Drunken Jack's with live music. (843) 651-2044.
Flo's Place Restaurant and Raw Bar. (843) 651-7222.
Kyoto Japanese Steak House. (843) 651-4616.
Seafare Seafood Restaurant. (843) 651-7666.

Surfside
The Charleston Café. Reservations are recommended. 815 Surfside Drive, Surfside Beach. (843) 238-2200.

The Good Times. 700 Business Highway 17, Surfside Beach. (843) 238-3211.

Fenway Park, a sports bar and restaurant. 118 South Ocean Boulevard. (843) 828-1111.

Litchfield
Litchfield Beach Fish House. (843) 237-3949.
Calypso Beach Bar & Grill. (843) 237-4211.
Hanser House Family Restaurant is open seven days a week for lunch and dinner; breakfast is served on weekends. (843) 235-3021.

Pita Rolz offers numerous signature sandwiches, hand-dipped ice cream, and fresh fruit smoothies. (843) 235-3338 and www.pitarolz.com.

The Mayor's House Restaurant. (843) 237-9082.
Webster's Fine Food & Spirits. (843) 237-3000.

SHOPPING
Pawley's Island is known for its handmade rope hammocks found at **The Hammock Shops**. There are about two dozen shops that surround the original Pawley's Island Hammock Shop including a candle shop, a book and stationery store, a nature store, a gourmet food store, a jewelry store,

Pawley's Island is known for its handmade hammocks. Terrance Zepke

a general store of gifts and collectibles, a Christmas shop, and several others. Highway 17, Pawley's Island. (843) 237-8448, (800) 232-8004, and www.hammockshop.com.

The Island Shops are across the street from The Hammock Shops. These stores carry specialty items, such as designer apparel, cookware, handicrafts, and gifts.

The Shops At Oak Lea and **Town Square**. These shops sell jewelry, china, footwear, clothing, unique pet gifts, and home furnishings. Highway 17, Pawley's Island.

Beach supplies, photo processing, hardware, and more can be found at **Pawley's Island Supplies**. At the corner of Highway 17 and North Causeway. (843) 237-2524.

If you're interested in Gullah handicrafts check out **The Gullah Ooman Shop**. It has an impressive collection of sweetgrass baskets, art, Gullah collectibles, story quilts, wood carvings, and books. Turn off Highway 17 on to Waverly Road then turn again on to Petigru Drive. (843) 235-0747.

ANNUAL EVENTS
Pawley's Island 4th of July Parade.
Festival of Music and Arts (September).
Atalaya Arts & Crafts Festival at Huntington Beach State Park (September).
Pawley's Island Annual Tour of Homes (October).
Annual Turtle Strut on Pawley's Island (October).
Festival of Music and Arts (October).
Seafood Festival at Murrells Inlet (October).
Senior PGA Tour Championship (November).
Hospice Festival of Trees (December).
Low country Candlelight Celebration at Murrells Inlet (December).

NEARBY POINTS OF INTEREST
Georgetown is only 20 miles away. See the section on Georgetown for more information.

TOURISM INFORMATION
Georgetown Chamber of Commerce. P.O. Drawer 1776, Georgetown, SC 29442. (800) 777-7705, (843) 546-8436, www.seaport-georgetown.com, and www.GeorgetownSC.com.

Pawley's Island-Litchfield Business Association. PO Box 192, Pawley's Island, SC 29585. (843) 235-2726 and (888) 228-0199.

Pawley's Island Town Hall Information Center. PO Box 1818, Pawley's Island, SC 29585. After crossing the causeway, visitors will see a small building on the left. Brochures detailing the location and brief history of each historic edifice on the island can be obtained here. (843) 237-1698.

Pawley's Island Visitor's Center. 264 Highway 17, Pawley's Island. (800) 777-7705.

Myrtle Beach Area Chamber of Commerce serves Horry & Georgetown Counties. 1200 North Oak Street, PO Box 2115. Myrtle Beach, SC 29578. (800) 356-3016, (843)-626-7444, and www.myrtle-beachlive.com.

DIRECTIONS & ACCESSIBILITY
Twenty-five miles south of Myrtle Beach via Highway 17 South and 20 miles north of Georgetown via Highway 17 North.

☞ NORTH, SOUTH, AND CAT ISLANDS (Yawkey Wildlife Preserve)

Population: uninhabited

Most of the islands near Georgetown are part of three protected areas: Santee Coastal Reserve (a 24,000-acre bird rookery), Cape Romain Wildlife Refuge, or Yawkey Wildlife Preserve. Yawkey Wildlife Preserve is comprised of three islands that are perched at the entrance to Winyah Bay: North, South, and Cat Islands. This preserve was established by Tom Yawkey, late owner of the Boston Red Sox baseball team. He was an outdoorsman and self-taught ornithologist. When he died, he left this land to the South Carolina Natural Resources Department. The 20,000-acre wildlife refuge endowment by Yawkey remains one of the biggest gifts of this type, not just in South Carolina, but in all of North America. The refuge is full of migrating shorebirds, wading birds, raptors, nesting bald eagles, wild turkeys, deer, rattlesnakes, and loggerhead turtles.

North Island is a fifteen-mile-long island that is situated at the mouth of the Winyah Bay, just 10 miles southeast of Georgetown. It is just a short boat ride away, but vegetation grows wild and there is no boat ramp or dock. Low tide restricts accessibility even more. The island is comprised of 934 acres of upland and 4,449 acres of marsh. Land has been cleared around the old lighthouse but the rest of the refuge remains untouched. An 87' lighthouse, presently known as Georgetown Lighthouse, was established on North Island in 1801. It was rebuilt in 1812 and 1867, because of damage sustained during a storm and the Civil War. The whitewashed beacon is operated by the US Coast Guard and was automated in 1986.

Marquis de Lafayette came to North Island in 1777, as Major Benjamin Huger's guest. The family was very much impressed with General Lafayette and his efforts on behalf of the colonists during the Revolutionary War. So much so that when Huger's son, Francis Huger, learned that Lafayette had been captured and was being held in an Austrian prison, he broke his hero out of jail. They made it to the border before being captured. Huger was detained for more than eight months in an Austrian prison for helping Lafayette escape.

Robert Francis Withers, who once owned North Island, lived on it with his family and left only when he had to attend to business at his plantation near Georgetown. On September 27, 1822, while he was on the mainland taking care of plantation business, his family drowned during a horrific hurricane. Over the years, many planters owned summer homes on North Island. Later, it was used for deer and duck hunts. While the island was owned by Confederate General Edward Porter Alexander,

❦ ❦ ❦

When International Paper Company built their plant and corporate headquarters in Georgetown in 1936, it was such a huge undertaking that construction workers had to be brought in from outside areas. Ultimately, a bordello was considered the best solution to keep the men out of trouble. Tom Yawkey was asked to help with the "Bordello Project." He found property on the outskirts of town and a madame to run the establishment. She accepted only the most promising young women and made them into lovely, refined ladies. The bordello was known as Sunset Lodge and as word of the fine brothel spread, clientele came to include sea captains, merchants, doctors, salesmen, and politicians. It is rumored that Tom Yawkey even brought business associates and friends, even some of his baseball players, to the brothel. Some took the girls out on their yachts for lengthy cruises to tropical places. Even though it was illegal, local authorities ignored Sunset Lodge until 1969, when the sheriff shut the brothel down without warning. Some say the wife of a politician or local businessman grew tired of her husband's extramarital activities and pressured the sheriff to address the problem. The girls were all sent packing, but the madam was allowed to stay. She lived there until her death. Future occupants swore her spirit haunted the dwelling, which burned down in 1992.

❦ ❦ ❦

President Grover Cleveland stayed briefly as his guest. The men went duck hunting, and the president got stuck in mud. The mud was so thick he couldn't be dragged out of it except by leaving his embedded boots behind. That spot on the island is referred to as the President's Stand.

Both North and South Islands were used as defense fortifications for Winyah Bay and Georgetown during the Civil War, and soldiers patrolled their beaches watching for the enemy. The island was purchased in 1911 by William Yawkey, a successful businessman and owner of the Detroit Tigers. He also bought Cat and South Islands and left them all three to his nephew, Tom, upon his death in 1919. Tom took over his uncle's enterprises and made the islands into a wildlife refuge during the 1960s. In addition to leaving the refuge to the South Carolina Wildlife Department upon his death in 1976, he left a $10 million fund for managing the Tom Yawkey Wildlife Center, which is an outdoor lab experimenting with the best ways to care for and supervise wildlife.

South Island is a 7,000-acre waterfowl preserve. It was once used as a summer haven for Georgetown area planters and their families. At one time, General E. P. Alexander owned it. During the time that William

Georgetown Lighthouse is on North Island,
a boat-access-only island in Winyah Bay.
Courtesy of Georgetown Chamber of Commerce

Yawkey owned the island, he constructed a hunting lodge on it, two club-houses, and a stable. Yawkey brought ball players, such as Ty Cobb and Tris Speaker to spend time on the island.

When his nephew, Tom Yawkey, assumed ownership of South Island, he built a large home to live in during winter months. Tom and his bride, Elise, never resided in the house. When the couple arrived and saw their new home, they decided they wanted something simpler. They moved into the hunting lodge and gave the big, elegant house to the superintendent of South Island Plantation. The couple later divorced and Tom remarried someone who was said to be more suited to his personality, Jean Hollander Hiller. They had a small ceremony at the Georgetown home of Leila and Ralph Ford. Tom and Jean wore hunting outfits while the Fords wore formal clothes. The Yawkeys came to their hideaway every year as soon as baseball season ended and stayed until spring training began. The lodge burned down one summer and Tom had two trailers moved to the island as soon as he heard the news. The Yawkeys never considered moving the superintendent out of the big house. Tom Yawkey died in 1976 and Jean Yawkey died in 1992. Both chose to have their ashes scattered around these islands they loved so dearly.

Cat Island, like most South Carolina islands, was once home to one or more Indian tribes. After Georgetown was founded, plantation owners took up residence on these islands. Some of the biggest rice plantations on Cat Island were White Marsh, owned by William Rivers Maxwell, and the Hume Plantation, owned by Alexander Hume. Traces of these places and bygone times can still be seen today through bamboo stands, ruins, and gravesites. The island was once owned by Mrs. William Gouveneur Ramsay of Wilmington, Delaware, who willed it to her daughter, Mrs. William E. Phelps, in 1927. Eventually, Tom Yawkey came into possession of it and built a church so that residents, who were slave descendants, would have a place to worship without having to journey to the mainland. St. James A. M .E. Church was once visited by the Archbishop of Canterbury.

The island lost power so often that Yawkey hired an engineer to put in a diesel generator. Despite Yawkey's warnings that the ferry used to transport islanders to the mainland was not sufficient for transporting the generator, the engineer argued it would accomplish the task. The obstinate engineer could not be persuaded to use a barge. Yawkey threw a party, inviting friends and the media to witness the failure he was sure would occur. While sipping champagne and consuming oysters, the group watched the engineer supervise the transfer of the generator onto the ferry. Halfway across the water, the ferry began sinking. Yawkey taunted the engineer by calling out, "Go down with the boat. Every good captain goes down with his boat!"

TOURS & ATTRACTIONS
Yawkey Wildlife Center offers free tours onboard a private ferry on Tuesdays 3 P.M.-6 P.M., year-round. Reservations are required and must be made at least three months in advance. For more information call the Yawkey Wildlife Center at (843) 546-6814.

A **Shelling and Lighthouse Cruise** is offered aboard the *Carolina Rover.* The excursion promises to take participants to the site of the Civil War wreck of the Union flagship *Harvest Moon,* to the best shell collecting on the Carolina Coast, and to the only tour of North Island to see Georgetown Lighthouse. The three-hour cruises include commentary by on-board naturalist. Summers only. Cruises depart from the boardwalk at the dead end of Georgetown's Broad Street. (800) 705-9063 and (843) 546-8822. $

NATURE & WILDLIFE
Conditions are ideal for migratory birds. Bald eagles nest here every winter.

DIRECTIONS & ACCESSIBILITY
See Tours & Attractions for ferry service information.

ᗡ CAPE ROMAIN WILDLIFE REFUGE ISLANDS

Population: uninhabited

Cape Romain National Wildlife Refuge (established in 1932) is 22 miles of barrier island and salt marsh that comprise a 64,000-acre refuge—one of the best in America. The Sewee Visitor and Environmental Education Center is operated by both the Cape Romain Refuge and the Francis Marion National Forest and displays exhibits about the refuge and the forest, including live red wolves and birds of prey. Visitors may also watch a short film and follow a trail that is well-marked with descriptive signs. **Cape Island** is 1,184 acres and is home to the biggest Loggerhead Sea Turtle Nesting Program in the state. The island is next to Lighthouse Island and Raccoon Key. It is 21 miles south of Georgetown off of Highway 17 and 22 miles north of Charleston off of Highway 17 and is accessible only by boat. Cape Island is not open to the public, nor is nearby White Banks Island, a set of isles often leased for clamming.

Named after the saltwater grass that covers the island's sandy shores, **Marsh Island** is part of the Cape Romain National Wildlife Refuge. From April to September, thousands of brown pelicans nest on the approximately ten-acre island. Additionally, this little island, located in the middle of Bulls Bay between Raccoon Key and Bull Island, is frequented by royal terns, sandwich terns, laughing gulls, tricolored herons, snowy egrets, oystercatchers, great white egrets, glossy ibis, black skimmers, and gull-billed terns. But the pelican is "king" of this island. Marsh Island is one of the largest nesting colonies for brown pelicans on the eastern seaboard. Because of DDT, a pesticide that was banned in the early 1970s, the brown pelican was considered an endangered species until the 1980s. The pelican population has slowly increased until it was taken off

Alligator basking on shore at Cape Romain Wildlife Refuge.
Terrance Zepke

the endangered list. Because Marsh Island is such an important pelican rookery, the island is closed to the public.

The only accessible island in the refuge, except by private boat, is **Bull Island** (both Bull Island and Bulls Island are considered acceptable). Visitors may opt to take a 38-passenger pontoon boat through the refuge. During the thirty-minute ride, you will see lots of wildlife and scenery and end up on Bull Island with time for independent exploration.

The first time white men saw this island was in 1670 when a couple of English ships briefly anchored at Bulls Harbor in order to obtain fresh water. Seewee Indians saw the vessel and rowed out to meet them. The first English owner of the island was John Collins, who was presented with the land by the Lords Proprietors. He passed it on to his heirs in 1707, and it eventually ended up with the Bull family.

A fortification for protection against pirates was built on the island in the early 1700s because Bulls Bay and the creeks behind Bull Island were sometimes used by pirates as hideouts. During the Revolutionary War, the British used the island as a supply depot and all edifices were destroyed by the British. What wasn't annihilated at that time was destroyed during the War of 1812 and the Civil War. As part of Reconstruction, freedmen were offered incentives to relocate to Bull Island, but they refused.

Records indicate that the Magwood family owned the island until 1921 when possession was assumed by Gayer Dominick. The New Yorker bought the land as a hunting retreat and transferred ownership to the US Fish and Wildlife Service in 1936.

At 5,018 acres, Bull Island is the largest island in the Cape Romain Wildlife Refuge. It is also the only wooded island in the refuge, so it has the most varied wildlife and maritime forest, including live oaks, pines, wax myrtles, cedar, bay, and palmettos. A big accomplishment of the refuge has been the red wolf breeding program. The wolves were reintroduced to the island in 1970 under the Endangered Species Act and an aggressive breeding program began in 1987. Bull Island is one of only two federal reserves with a Class One wilderness rating, the highest possible classification. The island contains 277 bird species, twelve amphibian species, twenty-four reptile species, and thirty-six species of mammals.

Bull Island is 3 miles from the mainland and is accessible only by boat. It is a remote six-mile long barrier island that has 16 miles of trails through maritime forest, marsh, and beach. There are no amenities, so wear good walking shoes and bring insect repellent, food, and water. Some exceptional examples of wildlife include red-tailed hawks, peregrine falcons, yellow warblers, wood ducks, alligators, bald eagles, red wolves, turkeys, loggerhead turtles (who come ashore during summer to lay their eggs), and white-tailed deer.

TOURS & ATTRACTIONS

Coastal Expeditions is a private ferry service that provides a trip to Bull Island, departing from Moore's Landing in McClellanville, 16 miles northeast of Charleston. Take Highway 17 North and turn right on Seewee Road. Make another right onto Bull Island Road and follow it about one mile until it ends at Moore's Landing. To reach Moore's Landing from Myrtle Beach, follow Highway 17 South for 75 miles or from Georgetown, proceed 33 miles south. Follow the signs for McClellanville. Public parking is free.

The refuge is open daily from sunrise to sunset. Cap'n Randy leads the trip that departs at 10 A.M. and 12:30 P.M., Monday-Friday and 10 A.M. only on Saturdays. Call to verify the departure days as they change periodically. Coastal Expeditions also offers kayaking adventures to Capers Island and Edisto River, an overnight in a treehouse in the preserve, and a Young Naturalists' Kayak Adventure Camp. They also provide instruction and rent kayaks and related equipment. 514-B Mill Street, Mt. Pleasant, SC 29464. (843) 881-4582 and www.coastalexpeditions.com. $

ACTIVITIES

There are no organized activities on the island. In addition to nature study and wildlife viewing, year-round sport fishing, hunting, clamming, oystering, and crabbing are permitted. No fires, pets, littering, weapons (except in hunting areas during hunting season), camping, or removal of any items found on the refuge are permitted. There is a small information station on the island.

ACCOMMODATIONS

BED & BREAKFAST INNS
Laurel Hill Plantation is a bed and breakfast on 8913 North Highway 17, McClellanville. (843) 887-3708.

CAMPING
Camping is not allowed on the refuge's islands but is permitted nearby at Francis Marion National Forest/Buck Hall Recreation Area. US 17 South, McClellanville. (843) 887-3257.

NEARBY POINTS OF INTEREST
McClellanville's Village Museum has exhibits depicting area history, including a Seewee Indian village, a Jamestown settlement, a look at Santee rice plantations, and the establishment of McClellanville. Interpretive tours, a gift shop, a picnic area, and a visitor information desk are available. 401 Pinckney Street. (843) 887-3030. $

Nature Adventures Outfitters, Inc. offers kayaking, canoeing, hiking, biking, and horseback riding trips through Francis Marion National Park. Trips are led by naturalists. Possible sightings include black bear, puma, bobcat, coyote, raptors, alligators, and wild boar. The outfitters also rent equipment, such as mountain bikes and tents. 1900 Iron Swamp Road, Awendaw (thirty minutes from Charleston). (800) 673-0679 and (843) 928-3316.

M & M Farms offers horseback riding in Francis Marion National Forest. Beginners and children are welcome. (843) 336-4886 and www.mmfarms.com.

ANNUAL EVENTS

Summer on Bull Island is very hot and humid with many insects. Spring and fall are the best times to enjoy the refuge. Many migrating birds can be seen in March and April. Alligators are often seen "sunning" on the banks of Upper Summerhouse Pond and Jack's Creek. Winter is hunting (deer and waterfowl) and fishing (channel bass, clamming, and oysters) season.

Annual Low Country Shrimp Festival (May) in McClellanville. (843) 887-3525.

DIRECTIONS & ACCESSIBILITY

The **Sewee Visitor and Environmental Education Center** is open 9 A.M.-5 P.M. daily except Mondays and holidays. It has a red wolf display and education area, trails, a gift shop, and an information center. 5821 Highway 17 North, Awendaw, SC 29429. (843) 928-3368. From Charleston, follow Highway 17 North for 22 miles. Follow the signs. Free.

See Tours & Attractions for ferry service information.

CHARLESTON
ISLANDS

CHARLESTON

Population: 100,122

Charleston County: 506,875

Charleston is actually a peninsula where the Ashley and Cooper Rivers meet to form the Atlantic Ocean—or so Charlestonians half-jokingly claim! Bedroom communities embody North Charleston, West Ashley, and East Cooper, which includes Mt. Pleasant, Sullivan's Island, and Isle of Palms.

Founded in 1670 and originally named Charles Town, after King Charles II, Charleston is one of the most interesting and historic cities in the United States. For example, the intersection of Meeting and Broad Streets is called the "Four Corners of the Law" because every legal requirement can be done at this junction. On one corner is St. Michael's Episcopal Church, where couples may get married; the next corner is the Charleston County Court House, where couples may pay taxes on their new home; the next corner is City Hall, where couples may file for divorce; and across the street on the fourth corner is the post office, where newly divorced couples may submit change of address forms! There are 2,800 historically significant buildings in the Charleston area.

Many refer to Charleston as the "City of Firsts" because the first shot of the Civil War was fired in the Charleston Harbor at Ft. Sumter, and Charleston boasts the world's first successful submarine attack during a Civil War blockade of the harbor in 1864. The vessel, *H. L. Hunley,* was excavated in 2000 and a museum is being built to contain the sub and its artifacts. Charleston also had the country's first golf course, Harlston Green (1786), Jockey Club (1836), historic zoning ordinance (1931), passenger train (1830), railway mail service, prescription drug store, and the

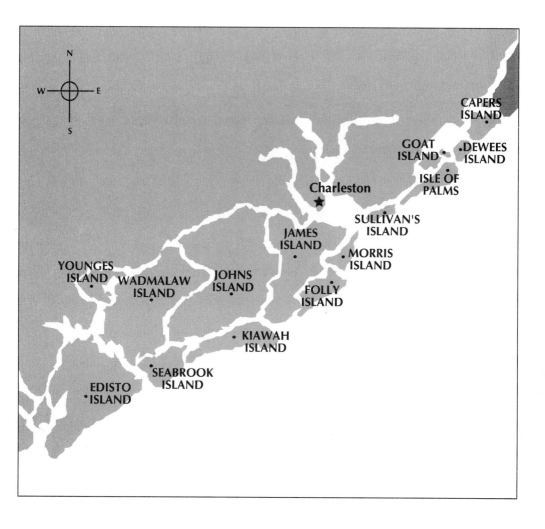

Welcoming Gateway Courtesy Charleston Convention and Visitor's Bureau

nation's oldest Chamber of Commerce (1773). The chamber was formed one night at Mrs. Swallow's Tavern on Broad Street by some businessmen who were concerned about a resolution regarding tea shipping. Charleston is also home to our nation's first science museum (1773), as well as America's first public museum, The Charleston Museum (1773), and the first structure built in this country for theatrical productions, the Dock Street Theatre (1735).

The first rice crop ever planted in America was grown in Charleston. The first female artist, Henrietta Johnston, hailed from this port city, and Dr. John Lining made our nation's first scientific weather observations from his house on King Street (1737). Furthermore, it was the origin of many southern trends and accomplishments. The South's first music store opened in Charleston on King Street in 1819 and operated until 1970. The South's oldest library was established here in 1748 and Charleston is also home to the state's first newspaper, the *South Carolina Gazette* (1732).

It is also known as "The Holy City" because you will almost surely get dizzy trying to count all the spires and steeples. Architecture and history buffs will be intrigued by these edifices. For example, the French Protestant Huguenot Church serves as an excellent representation of Gothic-style construction. Beth Elohim is the oldest reform synagogue in

❦ ❦ ❦

Charleston, February 7, 1812.

Yesterday morning, about half past three o'clock the inhabitants of this place were very much alarmed by another tremendous shock of an Earthquake. About a minute before the shock commenced, a loud sub-terraneous noise was heard resembling that made by a heavy loaded wagon running over frozen ground. The concussion began moderately, but soon became extremely violent, continuing with sudden jerks. The houses continued to shake about 25 minutes, sometimes with such extreme violence that many were apprehensive of their falling down. One chimney was thrown down and several bricks shook off of others; and several houses in town were considerably cracked.

Printed and sold at the [Boston] Printing Office.

❦ ❦ ❦

the country and considered the oldest synagogue still in use today. St. John's Lutheran Church melted its tower bell to be used by Confederates as cannon balls during the Civil War, and George Washington attended a service at St. Philips Episcopal Church in 1791.

Many historical battles took place in and around the city. It was held by the British during the American Revolution from 1780 to 1782. Queen Anne's War, the Yamasee Indian War, the War Between the States, and both World Wars took their toll on the city. The city was annihilated during the Civil War, not once but twice. First, when General Robert E. Lee arrived to defend the city, two slaves cooking dinner over an open fire accidentally set a blaze that destroyed 540 acres. On February 17, 1865, Charleston fell and citizens set the city on fire rather than relinquish it to the Yankees. Charleston was punished after the Union won the Civil War because of its key role in the secession.

Pirates, such as the infamous Blackbeard and Stede Bonnet, often raided merchant ships entering and departing from this bustling port. And Mother Nature has done her share to wreak havoc on Charleston with hurricanes, tornadoes, floods, fire, the Great Earthquake of 1886, and the destructive boll weevil, which ended the growth and production of cotton and indigo.

It wasn't until the early 1900s that Charleston really began to bounce back from all these setbacks and show significant economic improvement. The US Navy established a base and the Charleston Air Force Base came about during World War II. Plantation owners who had been wiped out by the boll weevil turned to producing timber and phosphate, an organic fertilizer found in the area.

Broad Street is in Charleston's Historic District. Courtesy Charleston Convention and Visitor's Bureau

Today, Charleston is the state's second largest city. It is over 188 square miles and its downtown area encompasses nearly 8 miles. More than eight million tons of cargo pass through its port every year, making it the seventh largest cargo port in the United States. The College of Charleston, Medical University of South Carolina, The Citadel, Charleston Southern University, and Trident Technical College all bring in thousands of students from across the state and country.

But, Charleston's economy thrives primarily because of tourism. It is one of South Carolina's top tourism destinations. *Condé Nast,* a leading travel magazine, has named it one of the top ten US Destinations for more than eight years in a row. *Travel Holiday* and *Bride* have rated it among the top five romantic destinations in America. Many of its restaurants have been featured in respected publications, such as *Gourmet, Coastal Living,* and *Southern Living.* In 1995, tourism accounted for an estimated $1.5 billion dollars. In 1998, roughly eight million visitors came to enjoy its many wonders, such as historic Battery Park and Rainbow Row, a colorful 18th-century waterfront district that contains grand homes painted various pastel shades. These Charlestonian homes were built as hybrids of townhouses and country homes. Various influences include French (balconies and tiled roofs), Dutch (curving gables), West Indies (doorways and basement arcades), and English (Georgian architecture). Houses were built with porches that extend along whatever side of the house that best grabs the ocean breeze. After a terrible fire in 1740, using wood for any purpose other than window frames, shutters, and interior work was outlawed. Brick and stucco were typically painted pink, green, yellow, and blue so as to make the neighborhood look more inviting.

TOURS & ATTRACTIONS

The Audubon Swamp Garden is 60 acres filled with swamp birds, creatures, bridges, and boardwalks for exploration. (800) 367-3517, (843) 571-1266, and www.magnoliaplantation.com. $.

South Carolina Aquarium opened in late 2000. Located on Calhoun Street at Charleston Harbor, it has ten thousand creatures and sixty exhibits. (843) 720-1990 and www.scaquarium.org. $.

The Battery at White Point Gardens contains military relics and monuments. Located in the southernmost part of the city. The area around it contains mostly historic homes, such as Edmondston-Alston House (1825). It has been featured on *America's Castles* as a wonderful tribute to early 19th-century architecture and style. It is filled with beautiful rugs and paintings, as well as exquisite antiques and silver. Open daily to the public. 21 East Battery. (843) 722-7171. Free.

Charleston Museum is the oldest public museum in America. It contains many artifacts and exhibits relating to low country history, including a replica of the *H. L. Hunley*, which was used during a Civil War blockade of Charleston Harbor. Open daily except holidays. 360 Meeting Street, Charleston, SC 29403. (843) 722-2996 and www.Charlestonmuseum.com. $.

The Citadel Museum pertains to the history of The Military College of South Carolina and the Corps of Cadets from the early 1800s to present. The cadets conduct a dress parade every Friday at 3:45 P.M. when school is in session. On the Ashley River near Hampton Park. (800) 868-DAWGS, (843) 953-6726, (843) 953-5006, and www.citadel.com. Free.

The Confederate Museum is operated under the supervision of the Daughters of the Confederacy. It is in Market Hall at 188 Meeting Street and is closed for renovation. Until work is complete on the building, the artifacts are being displayed at 34 Pitt Street, weekends only. (843) 723-1541. $.

Ship captains returning from the West Indies used to bring pineapples to share with friends and family. We didn't have them here, so the tasty fruit was cherished. It has come to mean hospitality and friendship, which is why you'll spot pineapple finials on posts and gates outside many historic homes in Charleston, as well as other port towns.

❧ ❧ ❧

The real **H. L. Hunley,** the nation's first submarine, launched a successful assault on the *USS Housatonic* on February 17, 1864. Even though it was a victory for the Confederates, the ship sank afterwards and all nine men aboard died. The sub was raised near Sullivan's Island in 2000 and is on limited display in Charleston. Scientists are hoping the wreck will provide evidence to finally determine why the sub sank. From downtown Charleston, take I-26 West to the Spruill Avenue exit. Take a left onto Spruill Avenue and then a right onto McMillan Avenue. Warren Lasch Conservation Center (the former Charleston Naval Base), 1250 Supply Street, Building 255, North Charleston, SC 29405. (843) 723-9797 (Hunley hotline), (866) 866-9938 (ticket sales), and www.hunley.org. $.

❧ ❧ ❧

Gibbes Museum of Art displays art dating from the 1700s to the present. 135 Meeting Street. (843) 722-2706 and www.gibbes.com. $.

IMAX Theater offers a forty-five-minute film experience on a five-story screen with 12,000-watts of digital sound. Next door to the South Carolina Aquarium at the Charleston Harbor, IMAX offers ever-changing presentations. Open 10 A.M.-10 P.M. 360 Concord Street. (843) 725-IMAX and www.charlestonimax.com. $.

Old Exchange Building and Provost Dungeon on East Bay Street reveals over three hundred years of history pertaining to pirates, patriots, and presidents. This is where famous pirate Stede Bonnet was jailed before his execution. Displays include animatronic figures, which really bring history alive! 122 East Bay Street. (843) 727-2165 and www.oldexchange.com. $.

The Postal Museum is the oldest operated post office in the Carolinas. It is located in the old post office at the corner of Meeting and Broad Streets. (843) 722-2996. Free.

Visitors may also choose to see **Waterfront Park,** an eight-acre park and pier at Charleston Harbor.

Delight in touring more historic homes and buildings.

Calhoun Mansion. 16 Meeting Street. (843) 722-8205.

Heyward-Washington House. 87 Church Street. (843) 722-0354.

Joseph Manigault House. 350 Meeting Street. (843) 723-2926.

Nathaniel Russell House. 51 Meeting Street. (843) 724-8481.

Thomas Elfe House. 54 Queen Street. (843) 722-9161.

Dock Street Theatre built in 1736 and rebuilt in 1937. (843) 577-7400 or (843) 720-3968.

Rainbow Row Courtesy Charleston Convention and Visitor's Bureau

Aiken-Rhett House is Charleston's "most intact antebellum mansion and outbuildings." 48 Elizabeth Street. (843) 723-1159.

A ERIAL   T OURS
Flying High Over Charleston, Inc. offers three different aerial tours. 202 Commons Way, Goose Creek, SC 29445. (843) 569-6148. $.

C ARRIAGE   T OURS
Carolina Polo & Carriage Company, 16 Hayne Street, Charleston, SC 29401. (843) 577-6767 and www.charlestoncarriagetour.com. $.

Classic Carriage Tours, Inc. 10 Guignard Street, Charleston, SC 29401. (843) 853-3747 and www.classiccarriage.com. $.

Old South Carriage Company. 14 Anson Street, Charleston, SC 29401. (843) 723-9712. $.

Palmetto Carriage Works, 40 North Market Street, Charleston, SC 29401. (843) 723-8145 and www.carriagetour.com. $.

B US   AND   M INI - B US   T OURS
Adventure Sightseeing Tours offers several different tours. (800) 722-5394, (843) 820-9770, (843) 762-0088, and www.touringcharleston.com. $.

Sites and Insights Tours provides black history tours, plantation tours, and sea island tours. (843) 762-0051 and www.SitesandInsightsTours.com. $.

Charleston's Finest Historic Tours. (843) 577-3311. $.

Charleston Tours, Inc. 545 Savannah Highway, Charleston, SC

29407. (843) 571-0049 and www.charleston-tours.com. $.

"Doin' the Charleston" Tours, Inc. PO Box 31338, Charleston, SC 29417-1338. (800) 647-4487, (843) 763-1233, and www.do03thecharleston-tours.com. $.

Gray Line Bus Tours. PO Box 219, Charleston, SC 29402. (800) 423-0444, (843) 722-4444, and grayline@bellsouth.com. $.

Talk of the Towne. 2166 St. James Drive, Charleston, SC 29412. (888) 795-8199, (843) 795-8199, and www.charleston.net/com/townetalk. $.

Taylored Tours of Charleston. 1300 Lenevar, Charleston, SC 29407. (888) 449-8687, (843) 763-5747, and www.toursofcharleston.com. $.

Sea Island Tours by Sites & Insights Tours provides two-hour tours to James Island and Johns Island that include stops at Angel Oak, plantations, war sites, and island folklore sites. Tours of other islands can be arranged. Departs daily from Charleston's Visitor Center. PO Box 21346, Charleston, SC 29412. (843) 762-0051 and www.sitesandinsightstours.com. $.

WATER TOURS & CRUISES

Explorer Cruises offers dolphin-watching on its guided harbor and barrier island tours, as well as inshore fishing and crabbing. Departs daily from Mt. Pleasant's Shem Creek and Charleston Maritime Center. (843) 856-8761 and www.explorercruises.com. $.

Schooner Pride, Ltd. PO Box 1067, Johns Island, SC 29457. (888) 571-2486, (84) 559-9686, and www.schoonerpride.com. $.

SpiritLine Cruises offers harbor tours and dinner cruises with a good menu and sightseeing. 205 King Street, Suite 204, Charleston, SC 29401. (843) 722-2628 and www.spiritcruises.com. $.

Deep Sea Fishing aboard the *Silver Dolphin*. Captain Bill has more than forty years of experience. The boat is equipped with the latest technology and equipment. Departs daily from Ripley Light Marina. (843) 556-3526. $.

WALKING TOURS

Architectural Walking Tours of Charleston, 173 Meeting Street at the Meeting Street Inn, Charleston, SC 29401. (800) 931-7761. $.

Charleston by Foot. 316 Confederate Circle, Charleston, SC 29407-7431. (843) 556-0664. $.

Charleston Strolls Walk with History. PO Box 1651, Charleston, SC 29402. (843) 766-2080 and www.ccharlie.com. $.

Civil War Walking Tour. 17 Archdale Street, Charleston, SC 29401. (843) 722-7033 and www.civilwartours.com. $.

The Original Charleston Walks offers several of the "Best Tours in Charleston's History," ranging from historic homes walk to wicked Charleston. Open daily. (800) 729-3420, (843) 577-3800, and www.

charlestonwalks.com. $.

The Pirates of Charleston/Tour Charleston, LLC. (800) 854-1670, (843) 723-1670, and www.tourcharleston.com.

The Story of Charleston/Tour Charleston LLC. (800) 854-1670, (843) 723-1670, and www.tourcharleston.com. $.

Educational Tours by Charleston Strolls arranges programs and tours by appointment for all ages "first grade classes through Elderhostel." Established in 1979, they even offer foreign language guides and can make presentations, as well as give insightful tours. Topics include African-American heritage, antiques, churches and graveyards, eco-tours, ghost hunts, military history, plantation life, scavenger hunts, and more. P. O. Box 1651, Charleston, SC 29402. (843) 766-2080. $.

GHOST WALKS

Charleston's Best Ghost Walk is offered three times nightly. Reservations are required. (843) 819-4565. $.

Low Country Ghost Walk. Open year-round and offered three times nightly. (800) 729-3420. $.

On The Market Tours: Ghosts Walking Tour. Departs twice nightly from the steps of Market Hall at the intersection of Market and Meeting Streets. Reservations are required. (843) 853-TOUR and (843) 853-8687. $.

The Ghosts of Charleston/Tour Charleston LLC. (800) 854-1670, (843) 723-1670, and www.tourcharleston.com. $.

Ghost Walk. 122 Queen Street, Charleston, SC 29401. (843) 577-5931 and www.ghostwalk.net. $.

ACTIVITIES

There are many, many art galleries, bookstores, boutiques, and specialty shops in Charleston. But even visitors who aren't much for shopping won't want to miss the **Old Slave Market,** which is now a giant flea market filled with local craftspeople and merchants. Free.

M & M Equestrian Center is about twenty minutes from downtown Charleston. It offers rides through Francis Marion National Forest, horseback riding lessons, fishing, camping, and more. (843) 336-4886. $.

Palmetto Islands County Park is operated by the Charleston County Park & Recreation Commission. It contains Splash Island Family Waterpark, pedal boats, bike rentals, fishing and crabbing, playgrounds, and 943 acres of trails for walking and biking. 444 Needlerush Parkway, off Highway 17 at Mt. Pleasant. (843) 884-0832 and www.ccprc.com. $.

Tidal Wave Water Sports operates out of Charleston's City Marina and offers fishing charters, power boat rentals, eco-tours, parasailing, water-ski charters and lessons, jet ski rentals and safari tours, banana boat rides, kayak rentals, and nature tours. (843) 853-4FUN. $.

Charleston Municipal Golf Course. (843) 795-6517. $.

Patriots Point Links is approximately eight minutes from downtown Charleston at Mt. Pleasant on Charleston Harbor. (843) 881-0042 and www.patriotspointlinks.com. $.

Dunes West Golf Club is also at Mt. Pleasant and open to the public. It was voted one of America's Fifty Best Courses by *Golfweek* and ranked Top Ten New Resort Course by *Golf Digest* and *Golf Magazine.* (843) 856-9000. $.

Charleston National Country Club is a championship course located at Mt. Pleasant, designed by Rees Jones. The pubic is welcome. Rated as the number one non-resort course in Charleston area by *Golf Magazine.* (888) 915-5678. $.

Deep-sea fishing charters are available at **Shem Creek,** as well as nightlife, shopping, and dining. You'll find just about anything you desire on Coleman Blvd. There are also a couple of noteworthy attractions across the Shem Creek Bridge.

The **Museum on the Common** contains displays by local artists chronicling low country life. It also has an award-winning exhibit, "Hurricane Hugo Revisited" (one of the most devastating hurricanes to ever hit the area).

There's also a **Historic Old Village** filled with fine antebellum homes. The nearby Pitt Street Pharmacy is renowned for its milk shakes.

There are several **public boat landings** in North Charleston, Mt. Pleasant, West Ashley, and East Cooper. For more information, contact the Charleston County Park and Recreation Commission, Attn: Boat Landing Coordinator, 861 Riverland Drive, Charleston, SC 29412. (843) 795-BOAT.

Ashley Marina. 33 Lockwood Boulevard. (843) 722-1996.

Bohicket Marina. 1880 Andell Bluff Boulevard. (843) 768-1280.

Buzzard's Roost Marina. 2408 Maybank Highway. (843) 559-5516.

Charleston Harbor Marina Resort. 24 Patriots Point Road. (843) 856-9996.

City Marina. 17 Lockwood Drive. (843) 723-5098.

Cooper River Marina, Charleston Naval Base. (843) 554-0790.

Mariner's Cay Marina. 3-A Mariners Cay Drive. (843) 588-2091.

Ripley Light Marina. 56 Ashley Point Drive. (843) 766-2100.

Tolers Cove Marina. 1610 Ben Sawyer Boulevard, Mt. Pleasant. (843) 881-0325.

ENTERTAINMENT & NIGHTLIFE

Charleston has a **Symphony Orchestra.** (843) 723-7528.

Charleston Riverdogs minor league baseball. (843) 577-DOGS and

(843) 577-3647. $.

Stingrays hockey. (843) 744-2248. $.

Charleston Battery soccer. (843) 971-GOAL and (843) 971-4625. $.

Midtown Theatre offers live performances. Call for current show offerings. 372 King Street at Calhoun. (843) 579-0075. $.

Nationally recognized **Charleston Stage Company** performs at the historic Dock Street Theatre. 133 Church Street. (843) 577-5967 and (800) 454-7093. $.

Footlight Players is the state's longest-running theatre company. Shows are in an 1850s' cotton warehouse turned theatre in Charleston's French Quarter. 82 Queen Street. (843) 722-7521 or (843) 722-4487. $.

Vendue Inn has a rooftop terrace bar and restaurant. 23 Vendue Range, downtown Charleston. (843) 723-0485.

Robert's of Charleston offers gourmet dining, premium wine selections, and entertainment. Broadway show tunes are played while you dine on exotic fare. 182 East Bay Street. (843) 577-7565.

Tommy Condon's Irish Pub, owned and operated by an Irish family, features live Irish music Wednesday–Sunday and stays open late. It also serves a seafood menu.160 Church Street at The Market. (843) 577-3818.

Vickery's Bar & Grill (now also on Shem Creek in Mt. Pleasant) offers patio dining, a lounge bar, late-night dining, and American fare with a Cuban influence. It has won best recipe, best patio, best bartender, best martini, and best happy hour at the Oyster Festival. Good atmosphere, eclectic clientele, extensive beer and wine selections, and tantalizing desserts. 15 Beaufain Street. (843) 577-5300.

Mandalay is a three-story micro-brewery complete with open kitchen that offers "the finest wood-fired pizza in town." 275 King Street.

Southend Brewery & Smokehouse has live entertainment nightly and diverse menu, including baby back ribs. 161 East Bay Street. (843) 853-4677.

The Indigo Lounge is a premier dance club. Located in the historic district, it is equipped with couches, mahogany bars, and palm trees alit with tiny white lights. Open Wednesday-Sunday. 5 Faber Street. (843) 577-7383.

Club Tango. 39 Hutson Street in the Camden Exchange Building. (843) 577-2822.

ACCOMMODATIONS

Doubletree Guest Suites. (800) 527-1133 and (843) 577-2644.

Charleston Hilton North. (800) 445-8667 and (843) 747-1900.

Westin Francis Marion Hotel and Spa Adagio on King Street. (800) 433-3733 and (843) 571-1000.

Embassy Suites on Meeting Street. (800) 362-2779 and (843) 723-6900.

Best Western King Charles Inn circa 1830. (800) 528-1234 and (843) 723-7451.

Charleston Place Hotel on Market Street. (800) 611-5545, (843) 722-4900, and www.charlestonplacehotel.com.

Comfort Inn. (843) 577-2224.

Days Inn. (843) 723-8411.

Holiday Inn. (843) 805-7900, (843) 556-7100, and www.charleston-hotel.com.

Best Westerns. (800) 528-1234.

Sleep Inn. (800) SLEEP-INN and (843) 856-5000.

Hampton Inn. (800) HAMPTON, (843) 723-4000, and www.charleston-hotels.net.

Some locally-owned motels include:

Lord Ashley Motel. (843) 766-8885.

Mills House, circa 1853, is conveniently located on the corner of Meeting and Queen Streets and offers deluxe rooms and suites. (800) 874-9600, (843) 577-2400, and www.millshouse.com.

Catalina Inn. (843) 747-3663.

BED & BREAKFAST INNS

1837 B&B and Tea Room. (843) 723-7166)

Battery Carriage House Inn. (800) 775-5575 and (843) 727-3100.

Fantasia B&B. The Mary Scott House, circa 1813. (843) 853-0201 and www.fantasiabb.com.

Harbourview Inn overlooks Charleston Harbor. (843) 853-VIEW, (843) 853-8439, and www.harbourviewcharleston.com.

31 East Battery Street. (843) 723-2841 and bbonline.com/sc/zerowater.

Vendue Inn on Vendue Range is near Waterfront Park. (800) 845-7900 and (843) 577-7970.

The Palmer Home on East Battery. (888) 723-1574 and (843) 853-1574.

John Rutledge House Inn. (800) 476-9741 and (843) 723-7999.

The Kitchen House on Tradd Street has been written up in many magazines. (843) 577-6362.

Meeting Street Inn. (800) 842-8022 and (843) 723-1883.

Planters Inn overlooks the Old Market. (800) 845-7082.

The Cannonboro Inn is on Ashley Avenue. (843) 723-8572.

Victoria House Inn on King Street. (800) 933-5464.

Governor's House Inn on Broad Street is the former governor's mansion and is on the National Register of Historic Places. (843) 720-2070 and (800) 720-9812.

The Jasmine House is an 1843 Greek Revival Mansion located on Hasell Street. It has a private courtyard and Jacuzzi. (843) 577-5900 and www.aesir.com/jasminehouse.

There is also **Bed, No Breakfast Guest Rooms** in the historic district. It has very reasonable rates and has been written up in the *New York Times* as "no frills but pleasant." (843) 723-4450.

Many Charlestonians have made bed and breakfasts out of their luxurious Battery Park homes. (800) 853-8000 and (843) 853-8000.

There is also a registration service, Historic Charleston Bed & Breakfast, that represents approximately 50 privately owned houses and carriage houses. (800) 743-3583, (843) 722-6606, and www. charleston.net/com/bed&breakfast.

CAMPGROUNDS

KOA Campground offers a "beautiful, lakeside setting on an antebellum plantation. Fully stocked convenience store, showers, laundry, game room, recreation hall, heated pool, boat and bike rental, Kabins, Kottages, mini-golf and more!" Eight miles to downtown Charleston. (800) KOA-5796, (843) 849-5177, staykoa@aol.com, and www.advantagecharleston.com/koa.

RESTAURANTS

The world-renowned culinary school Johnson and Wales University is in Charleston. Many graduates choose to remain in the Charleston area, which is one reason the cuisine is so outstanding here. There are too many remarkable restaurants, cafés, bistros, and grills in Charleston to mention. But for those looking for authentic low country cuisine, here are some worthwhile dining experiences. Reservations are recommended and dress is resort casual.

Most seafood served at **Anson's** is caught daily in Charleston waters. Dinner is served in an elegant Southern dining room. 12 Anson Street. (843) 577-0551.

82 Queen Street has won best city restaurant for two years in *Southern Living's* Readers' Choice Awards. Specialties include Charleston spiced oysters, she-crab soup, fried green tomatoes, Charleston bouillabaisse, shrimp and crawfish jambalaya, pan-fried McClellanville crabcakes, and peach praline cobbler. Open every day of the year. A light menu is served between lunch and dinner, and there is a Sunday brunch. 82 Queen Street. (800) 849-0082, (843) 723-7591, and www.82queen.com.

Also favorably reviewed in *Southern Living* is **Magnolia's**. Open daily for lunch and dinner. 185 East Bay Street. (843) 577-7771 and www.magnolias-blossoms.com.

Another award-winning restaurant is the **Charleston Grill**, featuring live jazz nightly. Casual, elegant attire. 224 King Street. (843) 577-4522.

High praises have been sung by reviewers regarding **Circa 1886**. *The*

Post & Courier gives it five stars and *Food and Wine* swears it is Charleston's best-kept secret. 149 Wentworth Street. (843) 853-7828.

Poogan's Porch has been written up in *Gourmet, Bon Appetite,* and *Cuisine* magazines. It is also reportedly haunted! Open daily for lunch and dinner with Sunday brunch. 72 Queen Street. (843) 577-2337.

The Library at Vendue Inn is a four-star restaurant that serves low country cuisine and house-made desserts. 23 Vendue Range, downtown Charleston. (843) 723-0485 and www.vendueinn.com.

Hyman's, established in 1890, was voted the number one seafood restaurant in the state in a survey conducted by *Southern Living* and it has been featured in over thirty publications. Located in an old warehouse, the dress and atmosphere are definitely casual. Fresh seafood selections daily with dozens of fish and many shellfish to choose from. Open daily for breakfast, lunch, and dinner. Some interesting items include Sarah's okra gumbo, 13-bean soup, sautéed mussels, salmon and grits, and po-boy sandwiches. 215 Meeting Street. (843) 723-6000.

If you're looking for a great waterfront view and the best salad you've ever eaten with honey-butter croissants to die for, try **California Dreaming**. It has a vast menu selection, ranging from prime rib to the house specialty, baked potato soup. 1 Ashley Pointe Drive. (843) 766-1644 and www.californiadreaming.com.

Locals have chosen **A. W. Shucks Seafood Restaurant & Oyster Bar** as the best seafood in The Market. Don't miss their seafood casserole! 35 Market Street. (843) 723-1151 and www.a-w-shucks.com.

Kaminsky's is a good stop for those who enjoy gourmet coffee selections and desserts. It even offers a lowfat cheesecake for those watching their weight! It has been voted as the best in Charleston for desserts and milkshakes. Also located in Mt. Pleasant on Johnnie Dodds Boulevard. 78 North Market Street. (843) 853-8270.

Café Café has gotten rave reviews by *USA Today* for their homemade soups and desserts. They also serve cocktails and specialty coffees. Open daily. 177 Meeting Street at the corner of Market Street. (843) 723-3622.

Jestine's Kitchen is known for its delicious iced tea, called "Jestine's Table Wine" by locals. Restaurant founder, Jestine Matthews, died in the late 1990s at age 112. 251 Meeting Street. (843) 722-7224.

Bubba Gump Shrimp Co. Restaurant & Market is at 99 South Market Street. (843) 723-5665 and www.bubbagump.com.

Sticky Fingers has been voted Charleston's best for ribs, barbecue, and family dining. 235 Meeting Street and in Mt. Pleasant and Summerville. (843) 853-7427.

FESTIVALS & ANNUAL EVENTS
Low Country Oyster Festival (January).

Citadal Dress Parade (January). There are dress parades at the Citadel

every Friday afternoon when school is in session. Open to the public and free.

Festival of Homes and Gardens (March).

Blessing of the Fleet (April).

Lowcountry Cajun Festival (April).

Spoleto Festival USA (May).

Cooper River Bridge Run gets about 25,000 participants each year (April).

Scottish Highland Games at Boone Hall Plantation (September).

Autumn Fest & Greek Fest (October).

Taste of Charleston at Boone Hall (October).

Halloween Ghost Walk (October).

Air Force Air EXPO on base (October).

Candlelight Tours of Homes and Gardens and Afternoon Garden Tours and Teas, sponsored by Preservation Society of Charleston (October).

WorldFest Charleston Battle of Successionville at Boone Hall (November).

Holiday Tour of Homes (December).

Mt. Pleasant Christmas Parade (December).

NEARBY POINTS OF INTEREST

Boone Hall Plantation is America's most photographed plantation. This 738-acre estate contains formal gardens and slave quarters and has been used by many television and film crews. As soon as you enter the great iron gates, you'll see half of a mile of oak trees that lead up to the stately house. (843) 884-4371. $.

Caw Caw Interpretive Center is 654 acres filled with 7 miles of historical and interpretive trails, swamp boardwalks, and wildlife, such as deer, otter, American bald eagle, alligator, and songbirds. The interpretive center contains exhibits. Open Tuesday–Sunday, year-round. 5200 Savannah Highway (on Highway 17 South). Ravenel. (843) 889-8898. $.

Charles Towne Landing State Historic Site was the first permanent English settlement in South Carolina (1670) and is now a historic site and nature preserve. It is 3 miles northwest of Charleston, off SC 17. www.southcarolinaparks.com. $.

Cypress Gardens is about thirty minutes from Charleston and has foot paths, three picnic shelters, gift shop, aquarium, and butterfly house. Visitors may rent flat-bottomed boats or take a guided boat tour of the swamp. 3030 Cypress Gardens Road, Moncks Corner. (843) 553-0515 and cgardens@bellsouth.net. $.

Drayton Hall Plantation is the only house on the Ashley River to survive both the Revolutionary and Civil Wars. Nine miles northwest of downtown Charleston. (843) 769-2630 and www.draytonhall.org. $.

Magnolia Plantation and Gardens rewards visitors with a myriad of activities, such as the nature train and boat tour, a wildlife observation tower, a horticultural maze, a petting zoo, and the Barbados Tropical Garden. Pets are welcome. Ten miles northwest of Charleston. (800) 367-3517, (843) 571-1266, and www.magnoliaplantation.com. $.

Middleton Place is an 18th-century plantation that is also a National Historic Landmark. There is a restaurant on site that is open for dinner. Reservations are required. Fourteen miles northwest of Charleston. (843) 556-6020 and www.middletonplace.org. $.

Daniel Island is actually a bedroom community of greater Charleston. It is surrounded by Beresford Creek, Wando, and Cooper Rivers. It has a nature preserve, walking trails, waterfront park, Family Circle Tennis Complex with seventeen courts, and the Daniel Island Club, which has a private golf course and Golf Learning Center open to the public. Blackbaud Stadium, where Charleston's professional soccer team plays and concerts are held, is on Daniel. There are several different neighborhoods with homes ranging from golf villas to townhouses. Daniel Island Real Estate, 101 River Landing Drive, Charleston, SC 29492. (800) 958-5635, (843) 971-7100, and www.danielisland.com.

Bird Island has the largest wading bird colony in South Carolina. Here you'll see white ibises, cattle egrets, great egrets, tri-colored herons, and anhingas. It is accessible only by boat. Skiffs can be rented at Harry's Fish Camp on Lake Marion. Commercial tours are available. No one is permitted to visit March 1 through August 31. It is 19 miles west of Moncks Corner off SC Hwy 42 on County Road S-8-31. Moncks Corner Visitor Information. (843) 577-9549. Santee Cooper Property Management Division. (843) 761-4068.

Ft. Johnson Marine Resources Center is on the southern edge of Charleston Harbor. Wading birds, shorebirds, songbirds, migrating birds, and raptors can all be seen. Interpretive displays can be appreciated. (843) 795-6350.

Francis Bedler Forest is a 6,000-acre sanctuary in Four Holes Swamp. A one-and-a-half-mile boardwalk originates at the visitor's center. This swamp forest is home to many kinds of flora and fauna, as well as three hundred species of wildlife. Canoe trips, night walks, and more are offered seasonally. Reservations are required for these activities. Closed on Mondays. Pets and camping are not permitted. Forty miles northwest of Charleston. 336 Sanctuary Road, Harleyville, SC. (803) 462-2150. Free.

TOURISM INFORMATION
Parking in Charleston is very limited, so once you find a space, walk-

ing or taking the trolley is advisable. Be sure to ask if there is an additional fee for parking when you reserve accommodations.

Free publications can be found all over the greater Charleston area, including the Chamber of Commerce and Visitors Center. They typically offer discount coupons for tourist attractions and insightful articles.

Advantage Charleston is a publication with a calendar of local events, entertainment packages, restaurant menus and reviews, information and links pertaining to Charleston area, and more. (843) 884-2278, ext. 1234 and www.advantagecharleston.com.

Best Read Guide is a monthly publication that discloses special events offered each month, "hip hop spots," Charleston area maps, and entertainment, sightseeing, golf, and dining information. www.bestreadguide.com.

Charleston Gateway is a quarterly publication with an area map, and a calendar of events, plus shopping, sightseeing, dining, and golfing information. (843) 722-3969 and www.charlestongateway.com.

Charleston Area Convention & Visitors Bureau. The bureau has a "Forever Charleston" presentation, which gives visitors an overview of the city. DASH trolley passes and area attraction tickets are also available. Tourist packs can be obtained at the Visitors Center, requested online at www.touristpack.com, or picked up at any South Carolina Welcome Center. These free packets include a walking map of Charleston's Historic District, information on guided tours, and coupons to area restaurants and attractions. Also, ask about passes that provide discounted admission to many area attractions. 375 Meeting Street, across from the Charleston Museum. PO Box 975 Charleston, SC 29402. (800) 868-8118, (843) 853-8000, and www.charlestoncvb.com.

Charleston Metro Chamber of Commerce. Their website gives door-to-door directions and its maps and directions are printable. You may also request a free copy of the *Charleston Area Visitors Guide*. www.charlestonchamber.net.

North Charleston was incorporated in 1972 and is now one of the biggest cities in South Carolina. Both the Charleston International Airport and Amtrak station are in North Charleston. The city has a large coliseum, convention center, outdoor theater, public golf course, Old Village Historic Districts, Carolina Ice Palace with public ice skating, and a recreational center at Wannamaker County Park. North Charleston Visitor Center, 5001 Coliseum Drive. (843) 745-1090 and www.northcharleston.org.

MT. PLEASANT

Mt. Pleasant is just a bridge ride over the Cooper River from Charleston. Its earliest inhabitants were Sewee Indians. The tribe tried to cross the Atlantic Ocean in the early 1700s using canoes. They were trying to get to England, supposedly to trade goods with the English. They didn't make it. Although Mt. Pleasant was founded by settlers in 1680, it didn't officially become a town until 1837.

Something that shouldn't be missed is **Patriots Point Naval and Maritime Museum**. It is one of the biggest and best naval and maritime facilities in the world. It is home to the aircraft carrier *USS Yorktown*, submarine *Clamagore*, Coast Guard cutter *Ingham*, destroyer *Laffey*, and more. Visitors will also enjoy the Congressional Medal of Honor Museum, a Navy Flight Simulator that gives participants a five-minute ride on an F/A-18 with a mission to seek and destroy scud missile launchers in Iraq. Open daily. (843) 884-2727. $

Guilds Inn of Mt. Pleasant is a bed and breakfast with six guest rooms. It is a member of the South Carolina Bed & Breakfast Association. 101 Pitt Street. (800) 331-0510 and (843) 881-0510.

Long Point Inn is a bed and breakfast with five guest rooms. 1199 Long Point Road. (843) 849-1884.

MainStay Suites Patriots Point has a heated pool and fitness center, fully equipped kitchens, and a TV/VCR in every room. Pets are welcome. (800) 660-MAIN and (843) 881-1722.

Red Roof Inns. 17 North Bypass. (800) THE-ROOF.

Days Inn Patriots Point has over 130 rooms with a twenty-four-hour restaurant. (800) DAYS-INN and (843) 881-1800.

Comfort Inn has a gazebo with grills and picnic area. Pets are welcome. (800) 228-5150 and (843) 884-5853.

Shem Creek. Courtesy Charleston Convention and Visitor's Bureau

Microtel Inn & Suites lets kids stay free. (888) 771-7171 and (843) 971-7070.

There are two **Mt. Pleasant Visitors Centers**. One is in town at 100 Ann Edwards Lane, and the other is located inside the Hess Station at 291 Johnnie Dodds Boulevard/Highway 17. (843) 849-6154 and http://www.townof-mountpleasant.com.

DIRECTIONS & ACCESSIBILITY

From Columbia, take I-26 East and follow the signs to Charleston. The fastest route is I-26 East to US 78 East to US 52 South. The approximately 113 miles can be covered in just over two hours. From Myrtle Beach, take Highway 17 South and follow the signs to Charleston. It is approximately the same distance and duration.

By accessing the Charleston Chamber of Commerce website, visitors may get door-to-door directions. Enter your address and the address of the hotel or attraction you want to visit, and a map and printable directions will pop up within seconds. www.charlestonchamber.net.

Mt. Pleasant is separated from Charleston by the Cooper River. To get there, stay on Highway 17 and cross the Cooper River Bridges, or take I-526 from Charleston across the Wando River Bridge and the I-526 Mark Clark Expressway will take you across the town and intersect with Ben Sawyer Boulevard. Turn left to head toward Sullivan's Island and Isle of Palms or turn right and follow the signs to get to Patriots Point and Ft. Sumter Tour Boats. Water taxis can be hired to get you from Charleston to these beach communities. Shem Creek is often referred to as the historic heart of Mt. Pleasant. If you're interested in seeing it or dining in some of the outstanding waterfront restaurants, take Highway 17 to Coleman Boulevard, which brings visitors into Shem Creek.

CAPERS ISLAND

Population: uninhabited

Capers Island State Heritage Preserve is one of the few remaining undeveloped barrier islands in South Carolina. This 2,170-acre island

Capers Island Courtesy of South Carolina Department of Natural Resources

became a heritage preserve on December 16, 1977. According to the Division of Marine Resources Capers Island Heritage Preserve Management Plan, "The State of South Carolina through the Wildlife and Marine Resources Department purchased Capers Island from Citizens and Southern National Bank of South Carolina (as Trustee under the provisions of the Capers-Dewees Trust) in February 1975." This 3.3-mile-long and 1.4-mile-wide island contains salt marsh, beach, and maritime forest. Exotic plants include the Chinese tallow tree and the French tamarisk. Most of South Carolina's shorebirds and wading birds can be found here, such as American oystercatchers, ospreys, eagles, birds of prey, songbirds, and loons. Manatees, bottle-nosed dolphins, and loggerhead sea turtles have been seen around the island. Loggerhead sea turtles once nested on the upper beach but rarely come to Capers nowadays because of loss of the dunes. According to the Department of Natural Resources, there are bobcats, alligators, snapping turtles, tree frogs, lizards, chameleons, skinks, minks, river otters, and diamondback terrapins. There used to be wild hogs, cattle, and sheep, but they disappeared from the island in the 1980s. Some visitors claim to have seen black bears and bobcats, but these sightings have not been confirmed by rangers.

According to the Marine Resources Office, more than 10,000 people visit the island annually and most are day-trippers as opposed to campers. This is a popular spot in the summer. Area residents paddle over to sun, picnic, and camp. Although there's not much here, it is a pretty and serene place to spend a day or two, especially for beachcombers and fishermen.

South Carolina is serious about keeping places like Capers Island natural and unspoiled. The state is very protective of indigenous plants and wildlife. Local basket weavers are issued permits by the state for islands where the sweetgrass plants grow, including Seabrook and Capers.

Capers, known as Sessions Island from 1675–1705 and Capore Island until 1722, was one of many sea islands the King of England proclaimed for the Crown upon discovery. He later issued land grants to colonists who grew indigo, Sea Island cotton, and, later, corn, sugar cane, celery, asparagus, cauliflower, snap beans, melons, peaches, strawberries, blackberries, beets, and carrots.

Ownership of the island changed hands nearly a dozen times from 1868 until the time the state acquired it in 1975. The Huyler family owned it from the 1920s to the late 1950s. They spent winters on Dewees Island, which they also owned. This very fertile island was named after Bishop William Theodotus Capers of the Methodist Episcopal Church South and his son, General Ellison Capers, C. S. A., who became Bishop of the Episcopal diocese, in honor of their role in state history.

Today, Capers, like many state islands, is facing a substantial erosion problem, especially on the southeast end of the island and front beach.

ACTIVITIES

Bird-watching, wildlife photography, six miles of narrow trails for hiking and walking, and beach activities, such as sunning and shelling are available. No hunting is allowed.

There are a couple of Indian shell mounds, which consist of oysters, whelks, clams, and periwrinkles, on the southwestern tip of the island. The Sewee Indians had a village near Bulls Bay and a fort near the west side of Toomer Creek in 1685.

NATURE & WILDLIFE

Barrier Island Ecotours offers a three-and-a-half-hour nature exploration and boat trip led by a marine biologist, including shelling and bird-watching. During the excursion, visitors may spot pelicans, osprey, bottlenose dolphins, and more. Barrier Island Eco-Tours also has a two-hour sunset tour, complete with hors d'oeuvres. (843) 886-5000 and www.nature-tours.com.

Coastal Expeditions offers kayaking adventures to Capers Island, including overnight camping on the beach. They also offer instruction and rent kayaks. Shem Creek Maritime Center, 514-B Mill Street, Mt. Pleasant, SC 29464. (843) 884-7684 and www.coastalexpeditions.com.

CHARLESTON ISLANDS

Isle of Palms.

Sullivan's Island.

TOURISM INFORMATION

Information about the preserve, rules and regulations pertaining to it, and a beachfront primitive camping permit can be obtained from the **Department of Natural Resources** (843-762-5000). Those applying for camping permits will receive a list of regulations that must be adhered to for Capers Island. The Capers Island dock may be used to unload, but boats should be moored away from the dock. A wildlife ranger resides on the island in case of an emergency. Low tide during spring and fall is best for observing birds.

DIRECTIONS & ACCESSIBILITY

Capers is just north of Dewees Island and 15 miles northeast of Charleston. It is accessible only by boat since it is 3 miles out from the mainland and is one in a chain of protected barrier islands, along with Cape Romain Wildlife Refuge, Santee Coastal Reserve, and the Tom Yawkey Wildlife Center. It is bounded on the north by Santee Pass and Capers Creek, on the east by Price's Inlet and property of the Magwood family, on the south by the Atlantic Ocean, and on the west by Capers Inlet and Capers Creek. The nearest public landing is Moore's Landing at McClellanville (available during daylight hours at high tide) and Wild Dunes Marina at Isle of Palms.

☜ DEWEES ISLAND

Population: about 350 seasonal inhabitants

This island has accommodated Indians, Revolutionary War soldiers, rice planters, Civil War blockade-runners, vacationers, and residents for centuries. According to records, the island was intended to be a part of

*Mr. and Mrs. Huyler relaxing on the porch of their
Dewees Island home.* Courtesy of Dewees Island Development

the Christ Church Parish by order of the British sovereignty. There are shellfish remains, discarded by early island inhabitants, dating back as far as 2,000 B.C. A document written in 1697 reveals that the island belonged to Colonel Thomas Carey, who had served as Receiver General of the Lord's Proprietors and Deputy Governor of North Carolina. He was deeded the island as a reward for his service to the British Crown. At that time, the island was called Timicau and was used primarily for hunting.

*Mr. Huyler used this makeshift barge to transport his car
to Dewees.* Courtesy of Dewees Island Development

The Aggie Gray *is the private passenger ferry that delivers residents to* Dewees. *Terrance Zepke*

During the American Revolution, a British fleet was spotted from Dewees and adequate warning was given to prevent a surprise assault. Residents also participated in the war effort by supplying wood to troops stationed at Charleston. Despite all endeavors, Charleston fell to the British in 1780. William Dewees was expelled from the city at the end of the following year because he refused to accept British rule. He moved to Dewees and lived there until his death in 1786. The island is called Dewees in his honor.

In the early 1800s, the island was owned by Elizabeth Deleisseline and John Lewis Poyas. Deleisseline owned the southern side and Poyas possessed the northern end. The land passed on to their heirs for the next century until the Huyler family (of the Huyler Candy Company) bought Dewees and Capers Islands in the early 1920s. They were New Yorkers who came south because their five-year-old son, Jack, had a respiratory ailment that the doctors felt would improve in a warmer climate. They wintered on Dewees and summered in Wyoming. Mr. Huyler returned to the island in April 2000 to celebrate his eightieth birthday. Dewees was sold to the R. J. Reynolds family in 1952 to use as a hunting retreat.

The island saw its first real development in the 1800s when rice planters came to Dewees. After the end of that agricultural era, it was uninhabited once more until the 1970s. Three vacation homes were built on the southern tip by Robert Royall Jr., Edward Royall, and Robert "Bobby" Kennedy IV, but further development did not occur until 1991 when developer John Knott spearheaded efforts to create an intriguing balance of man and nature. In 1992, the Royalls, Kennedy, and Knott joined up with another investment group to form Island Preservation Partnership.

Because of its innovative marriage of nature and development, the island has almost assuredly been written up more than any other in the state. *The Wall Street Journal, The New York Times, Coastal Living, The State,* and many other publications have sung its praises. And I concur. It is the most harmonious mix I have ever witnessed.

According to the statement of philosophy found throughout Dewees Island literature, it is a "private, oceanfront island retreat dedicated to environmental preservation." It has been the recipient of many honors, including *Coastal Living's* Responsible Development Community Award and Keep America Beautiful National Award. According to IPP, only three percent of the 1,206-acre barrier island will be "invaded by construction," which means approximately only 150 homesites will be sold. Sixty-five percent of the island has been set aside as a nature preserve (350 acres) and over ninety percent of that portion will remain undisturbed. In other words, only 420 acres of the 1,206-acre island will be touched in any way.

While island life is laid back, environmental restrictions are not. No formal gardens or lawns are allowed. Gardening and landscaping must utilize native plants from a select list so as to preserve the soil and use mini-

The only attraction on Dewees is this old WWII watchtower.
Terrance Zepke

Another annual event is the "Wild Foods Harvest." Island naturalists and residents gather natural plants and herbs and learn ways to cook using them. Courtesy of Dewees Island Development

mal water. No cars are permitted on the island. Transport is by bicycle, electric golf carts, and walking. Homeowners must get permission to remove trees. No private boat docks are permitted, except for original island lots that are exempt from this policy. Only shared community docks are allowed. In fact, owners must relocate their boats within twenty-four hours to keep the island aesthetically pleasing. The same thing is true with golf carts at the landing. Homeowners call and announce their arrival time and the island transportation manager delivers their carts to the landing dock, or takes them back to a residence when an owner has departed.

Even on oceanfront lots, houses are set back into the trees, away from the beach. According to *S. C. Architecture*, "Some innovations being used at Dewees (such as breaking up roof lines to limit the massiveness of a house and make it complement the relatively low tree line on a barrier island) are being written into new design guidelines at Kiawah Island and elsewhere." Every house is designed and built to withstand severe storms and hurricanes. While there is no minimum size, a house cannot exceed 5,000 square feet.

Despite these stringent requirements and the higher cost of island construction, homesites are selling. When IPP started developing Dewees in 1992, land topped out at $267,000 for 3 oceanfront acres. As of fall 1999 those lots were listed at $1,250,000 and sold for $1,000,000. The

This oyster roast is just one of many events offered to island residents.
Courtesy of Dewees Island Development

mean age of homeowners is forty-four, roughly eighty percent hail from Georgia and the Carolinas, and many are permanent residents who work in Charleston.

Living on a boat-access-only barrier island is not for everyone, and the developer is the first to point that out. Those who are interested in living the principles set forth by the developer are best suited to Dewees.

TOURS & ATTRACTIONS
There is a World War II Submarine Tower, which was a vital part of Ft. Moultrie's defense efforts.

ACTIVITIES
The island has more than 2 miles of beach. Dewees claims it has the widest beach in South Carolina. Additionally, there is fishing, boating, tennis, basketball, volleyball, crabbing, sailing, exploring, nature walks on scenic trails, shrimping, biking, and swimming. An excellent example of Dewees' environmental measures is the community swimming pool. Rather than treat the water with chemical chlorine, table salt is converted through electrolysis into chlorine. The decking around the pool is a material that resembles wood but is actually manufactured from recycled plastic bags and bottles.

NATURE & WILDLIFE

The Landing Building, which houses meeting space and the post office, also contains the education center, the island's reference center. A full-time, in-resident naturalist regularly offers educational programs to local school groups and has designed hands-on learning programs for island families.

ENTERTAINMENT & NIGHTLIFE

Small satellite dishes are permitted for television reception and there are planned activities, such as oyster roasts at the oyster pit, photo contests, and parties.

ACCOMMODATIONS

There is a lodge that has rooms for property owners, their guests, or potential buyers, along with a dining room, a library, and a screened-in, wrap-around porch.

RESTAURANTS

There is a dining room at the lodge. Meals are served during special occasions but not on a regular schedule.

NEARBY POINTS OF INTEREST

Sullivan's Island.
Capers Island.
Cape Romain Wildlife Refuge.
Isle of Palms.
Charleston is only 12 miles south and about a 25-minute drive from Dewees Marina.

TOURISM INFORMATION

Dewees Island Real Estate, Inc. 46 41st Avenue, Isle of Palms. (800) 444-7352, (843) 886-8783, and www.deweesisland.com.

DIRECTIONS & ACCESSIBILITY

Non-residents should arrange a tour if interested in island living. There are guest facilities at the Huyler House for potential buyers. It is accessible only by boat. A private ferry shuttles residents and guests every hour from Isle of Palms and returns on the half hour. The trip takes just over twenty minutes. To get to Dewees Island Marina and Sales Office, turn right between the Isle of Palms Fire Station and the Isle of Palms Marina.

☞ GOAT ISLAND

Population: 30–35 permanent

The island was once owned by the Swinton brothers, who were given a land grant for it in 1732 by King George II. The island got its name from a couple, Mr. and Mrs. Goat, who once lived there.

At one time, Mr. Goat made a good living as a butcher in Charleston until his wife suffered a nervous breakdown. After that, she did all kinds of crazy things, such as standing in front of his store cradling a pig wrapped in a blanket and crying out to passersby to come look at her baby.

Greater Charleston Visitor Bureau Communication Assistant, Ryan McCants, told me that her grandmother knew Mr. and Mrs. Goat, but couldn't recall their real names. Mr. Goat used to scare the children because he was unkempt and behaved strangely. The pair, especially Mrs. Goat, was just too upsetting to those who lived on the island. Residents insisted he commit his wife, but he refused. Out of desperation, the couple took up residence on a small, uninhabited island where they raised their own food and a large herd of goats. This was how it became known as Goat Island.

The infamous bank robber Trigger Burke reportedly hid out on Folly Beach and Goat Island in 1957 before he was finally captured on Folly Beach. Some claim he hid part of the stolen money on the island, but no one has ever admitted to finding it.

Most residents are second-generation islanders. There are no cars or services on the island. Residents carry off their own trash and have private boats that transport them to nearby islands. One resident I spoke with works for Dewees Island Ferry Service. When she is scheduled to work or has business on the "mainland," she rows over to the Isle of Palms Marina. The trip can take five or thirty-five minutes, depending on the weather. She admits that this lifestyle can be inconvenient, especially for those who have children. At one time, the island was a bohemian retreat, populated by those wanting a less conventional lifestyle, but it is becoming more developed and upscale as others realize its potential.

TOURS & ATTRACTIONS

Blackriver Outdoors offers canoe and kayak rentals and naturalist-guided tours on the Black River. Day and evening excursions are offered at all skill levels, including beginners. Sample tours include Black River Cypress-Tupelo Swamps, Chicora Wood Plantation and Sandy Island Nature Preserve, Huntington Beach salt marsh creeks, Historic Georgetown Harbor (including around Goat Island). 21 Garden Avenue,

Highway 701 North, 3 miles north of Georgetown. (843) 546-4840 and www.blackriveroutdoors.com.

N E A R B Y   P O I N T S   O F   I N T E R E S T
Sullivan's Island.
Isle of Palms.

D I R E C T I O N S   &   A C C E S S I B I L I T Y
It is open to the public but there are no public amenities and access is by boat only. There is no public dock or marina; only small watercraft, such as dinghies and canoes, are useful.

✍ I S L E   O F   P A L M S

Population: 5,500

Past the eastern end of Sullivan's Island is a bridge that extends over Breach Inlet and connects to Isle of Palms. The island is 5 miles long, half a mile wide, and slightly larger than Sullivan's Island. Many speculate that Sullivan's Island and Isle of Palms, commonly referred to as Charleston's East Islands, were actually one island until a hurricane or nor'easter created the inlet that now separates the two.

The Seewee Indians were the first inhabitants of this 25,000-year-old island, formerly called Hunting Island and Long Island. Reportedly, the Indians swam out to meet the English settlers and carried them to shore. Legend has it that the Seewees were so taken with the English that they tried to row their canoes to England, but were all drowned at sea in severe storms. The truth is that the Indians, who traded animal furs and pelts with the English, felt they could get a better price by dealing directly with England. They figured their journey to England couldn't be far since so many English ships came and went from Charleston Harbor. They spent a year preparing for the trip by accumulating furs and pelts and by building dugout canoes with makeshift sails that could hold the men and their goods. The winds were favorable and all was well until a tropical storm

Isle of Palms Terrance Zepke

hit. Only a few men were spared, and they were sold as slaves by their rescuers. Those who were too young or sick to make the journey were eradicated by smallpox or joined other area tribes.

In 1791, a resolution permitting home building on the island was passed. A ferry service shuttled islanders to Charleston, but a couple of severe hurricanes hampered residential growth. Both natural disasters occurred during 1893 and resulted in many lost lives and homes. The island remained largely uninhabited until 1898 when it was bought by J. S. Lawrence, who envisioned it as a playground for wealthy Charlestonians and their friends. He renamed it Isle of Palms and built a fifty-room hotel with bathhouses, a restaurant, and a dancing pavilion. An amusement park, complete with a Ferris wheel and carousel, was added in 1912. A ferry, which left early in the morning, transported visitors from Charleston to Mt. Pleasant and a rail car took them the rest of the way via a single railroad bridge. They arrived at the resort by lunchtime. In 1929, the Grace Memorial Bridge, which connects the Charleston Peninsula to Mt. Pleasant, was built. In the mid-1940s, Isle of Palms was sold to developer J. C. Long of The Beach Company.

Long set up affordable housing for World War II vets and the island became a residential extension of Charleston. In those days, oceanfront lots sold for less than $2,000. Today, a one-week house rental can exceed that amount. Still, tourists flock to the island year after year to enjoy its 6 miles of beach. The population swells to well over 30,000 during the summer.

On the north end of Isle of Palms is the 1,600-acre Wild Dunes

Resort. The exclusive resort boasts championship golf courses and tennis courts that have been written up in many publications. It also has pools, a clubhouse, conference facilities, restaurants, and a reception center.

TOURS & ATTRACTIONS

Isle of Palms County Park is a 943-acre beachfront public park, with public beach access, pedal boat and bicycle rentals, picnic areas with grills, a playground, restrooms, vending machines, outdoor showers, and parking. The park is open daily. 114 Boulevard. (843) 886-3863 and www.ccprc.com. $.

ACTIVITIES

The Links Course, a par 72 course designed by Tom Fazio, was voted a *Golf Magazine* World's Top 100 course.

The Harbor Course. This par 70 course was also designed by Tom Fazio.

Wild Dunes Tennis Center has seventeen Har-Tru and two hard courts. The tennis clinics have been included in the top ten in the US by *Tennis Magazine* and ranked in the top five for kids tennis programs. Numerous villas have private courts, and there is a public court on 28th Avenue.

Island Fun Days Camp has kids' programs for children aged six and older. Activities include crabbing, a water park outing, a boat ride to Bull Island, a horseback ride through Francis Marion National Forest, and more. (843) 886-8294. $.

Ocean Park Shopping Center. 1400 Palm Boulevard.

Island Center. 1510 Palm Boulevard.

The Pavilion Shops. 1009 Ocean Boulevard.

The Isle of Palms Recreation Center has tennis courts, basketball courts, batting cages, a playground, and baseball and soccer fields. It also sponsors many year-round events and activities. 28th Avenue. (843) 886-8294.

Island Realty rents golf carts, beach chairs and umbrellas, kayaks, bicycles, and boats. They can also arrange parasailing, jet skiing, wave runners, and guided nature outings. 1304 Palm Boulevard. (800) 476-0400, (843) 886-8144, in Canada (800) 876-8144, info@islandrealty.com, and www.islandrealty.com.

Isle of Palms Marina, at the end of 41st Avenue, has boat slips that can accommodate vessels up to 120 feet in length. They also have charters, skiff rentals, a café, and a general store that sells groceries and fishing supplies. (843) 886-0209.

Wild Dunes Yacht Harbor. (843) 886-5100.

Long Island Yacht Harbor at Breech Inlet. Fishing is permitted at Breach Inlet, but not swimming.

Boating is a way of life at communitites such as Isle of Palms. Terrance Zepke

Parasailing, jet ski rentals, banana boat rides, fishing, and more can be accomplished through these companies:

Fishing Charters, Boat Rentals, Excursions & Tours. (843) 886-5100.

Tidal Wave Runners, Ltd. (843) 886-8456.

Lowcountry Boat Rentals. (843) 571-2628.

NATURE & WILDLIFE

A good spot for watching such birds as bald eagles, osprey, and great horned owls is around the Isle of Palms Connector Bridge. The island is a loggerhead turtle nesting area. Dolphins, deer, and pelicans can also be seen. Visitors will admire the island's live oak trees with Spanish moss draped over the branches, as well as the oleanders and crepe myrtles.

Barrier Island Ecotours offers nature exploration, including shelling and bird-watching, on nearby Capers Island with a marine biologist as a guide. Tours depart from the Isle of Palms Marina. (843) 886-5000 and www.nature-tours.com.

ENTERTAINMENT & NIGHTLIFE

The Windjammer has live entertainment nightly (rock n'roll). (843) 886-8596.

Edgar's has food and offers nightly entertainment (rock n'roll to country). (843) 886-2296.

ACCOMMODATIONS

The Boardwalk Inn in Wild Dunes Resort. (843) 886-6000.

The Seaside Inn. (888) 999-6516 and (843) 886-7000.

The Ocean Inn. (843) 886-4687.

Holiday Inn Express. (800) 465-4329, (843) 886-3003, and www.holidayinnisleofpalms.com.

Wild Dunes is a 1600-acre private resort on the northeast side of the island that offers championship golf courses, tennis courts, pools, a clubhouse, conference facilities, restaurants, and a reception center. In addition to hotel rooms, it offers homes for rent. There is a guard gate and the resort is not accessible to the general public. (800) 845-8880, (800) 886-6000, and www.wilddunes.com.

Great Beach Vacations–Isle of Palms. Guests receive a preferred guest amenity card and guide at check-in, which entitles the cardholder to discounts on green fees, bike rentals, cruises, charters, miniature golf, and more. The guide offers details about participating merchants, including addresses and a map. 1517 Palm Boulevard, Suite C, Isle of Palms, SC 29451-0159. (800) 346-0606, (843) 886-9704, info@isle-of-palms.com, and www.isle-of-palms.com.

Got a big group? How about renting "**The Castle**"? This oceanfront mansion sleeps eighteen to thirty. It has three living rooms, two kitchens, ten bedrooms with private baths, a large conference/dining table, an elevator, cable TV with VCR. Linens and maid service are available. 9040 Ocean Boulevard. Contact Ken Hancuff at (843) 886-8822 and khancuff@awod.com.

VACATION RENTALS

Beachside Real Estate. 1517-F Palm Boulevard. (803) 886-4056 and (800) 888-4056.

Carroll Realty, Inc. 103 Palm Boulevard. (803) 886-9600 and (800) 845-7718.

Charleston Resort Properties. 1507 Palm Boulevard. (803) 886-8600 and (800) 533-1343.

Prudential Carolina. 1400 Palm Boulevard. (877) 663-3456 and (843) 886-8110.

Dewees Island Real Estate. 46-41st Avenue, Isle of Palms, SC 29451. (803) 886-8783.

Dunes Properties. 1400 Palm Boulevard. (803) 886-5600 and (800) 476-8444.

J & A Properties. PO Box 789. (803) 886-7033.

East Island Real Estate. 29 J. C. Long Boulevard. (803) 886-8114 and (800) 338- 2301.

Gabriel Associates. PO Box 524. (803) 886-9805.

Island Realty & Sea Cabin Villas, including Wild Dunes and golf packages. 1304 Palm Boulevard. (803) 886-8144, (800) 476-0400, info@islandrealty.com, and www.islandrealty.com.

Resorts, Inc. 1116 Palm Boulevard. (803) 886-6493 and (800) 888-6493.

Wild Dunes Real Estate. 5757 Palm Boulevard. (803) 886-2500 and (800) 562-9453.

Ron Davis Realtors, LLC. 1507 Palm Boulevard. (843) 886-9500.

Destination Wild Dunes. 5757 Palm Boulevard. (803) 886-6000 and (800) 845-8880.

Hotel Marion. 916 Palm Boulevard. (803) 886-6493

Charleston Beach Properties. 1116 C Palm Boulevard. (888) 823-4744.

RESTAURANTS

All the restaurants on the island are casual in dress and atmosphere, and most are on Ocean Boulevard.

The Boathouse serves dinner nightly. Reservations are suggested. Lounge bar and entertainment are offered Sunday-Tuesday. (843) 886-8000.

Coconut Joe's Beach Grill and Bar offers live music on a rooftop deck. (843) 886-0046.

Edgar's features low-country cuisine and offers nightly entertainment (rock n'roll to country). (843) 886-2296.

Long Island Café patrons may choose simple or gourmet seafood dishes. (843) 886-8809.

One Eyed Parrot offers seafood prepared Caribbean style. (843) 886-4360.

Sea Biscuit Café serves breakfast and lunch from an American menu. (843) 886-4079.

ANNUAL EVENTS
Governor's Cup Bill Fishing Tournament (June).
Sand Shark 5K Beach Run (September).
Connector Bridge 10K Run (October).
Blues Extravaganza (February).

NEARBY POINTS OF INTEREST
Sullivan's Island.

TOURISM INFORMATION
Charleston Area Convention & Visitors Bureau. PO Box 975, Charleston, SC 29402. (800) 868-8118 and www.charlestoncvb.com.

Isle of Palms. Print out the free gift offer from their website, bring it to IOP City Hall, and receive a free souvenir t-shirt. PO Drawer 508. (843) 886-6428 and www.iop.net.

Mt. Pleasant/Isle of Palms Visitor Center. 100 Ann Edwards Lane or 291 Johnnie Dodds Boulevard/Highway 17 (inside Hess Station), Mt. Pleasant, SC 29464. (843) 849-6154 and www.townofmountpleasant.com.

DIRECTIONS & ACCESSIBILITY

Isle of Palms is 15 miles from Charleston and 8 miles from Mt. Pleasant. Take I-95 to I-26 towards Charleston. Exit I-526 towards Georgetown. Turn left at the stoplight and go one mile. Turn right onto SC 517 and proceed straight over the IOP Connector onto Isle of Palms, or take Highway 17 through Mt. Pleasant and cross the Ben Sawyer Bridge to Sullivan's Island and take Breach Inlet Bridge to Isle of Palms.

✍ SULLIVAN'S ISLAND

Population: 1,748

The island was discovered in 1666 by Captain Sandford, who claimed Charleston and all the surrounding areas for England. However, it is named after Captain Florentia O'Sullivan, who brought the first English settlers to the area aboard the *Carolina* in 1670. The island is about 3 miles long and only a quarter of a mile wide, yet it has played an important role in history. Before the jetties were built in the late 1800s, shifting sandbars made navigating the Charleston Harbor a very difficult task. Legislation was passed that authorized range lights and watchtowers on Sullivan's Island, and the island was primarily used to guide merchant ships into the harbor. Additionally, pilots were hired to safely guide ships in and out of the harbor.

Ft. Moultrie, on the northwest tip of the island, has always played a vital part in safeguarding Charleston. When Union troops had taken everything from Georgetown, South Carolina, to New Smyrna, Florida, everyone knew that once Charleston fell, the Civil War would be over. Ft. Moultrie is also the site of the first clear victory of the American Revolutionary War. This is pretty amazing considering the fort was fired

Fort Moultrie. Terrance Zepke

on by more than three hundred British cannons. The attack was led by Sir Peter Parker who was sent to seize Charleston and make it British headquarters. Not only did the palmetto log fort withstand the assault, Moultrie led a counterattack that annihilated the British. Edgar Allan Poe was stationed here for more than a year and as a result of the time Poe spent on Sullivan's Island he came up with the exciting tale *The Gold Bug*, which describes the escapades of a boy who spent a summer exploring the island.

In the 1700s, thousands of Africans arrived at Sullivan's Island because it was a debarkation point for the slave trade. The island was at the harbor entrance and was seemingly disease-resistant, therefore, slaves and cargo were brought here first for a quarantine period. Seminole Chief Osceola got sick and died while visiting the island and was buried near the fort. It was also where notorious pirate Stede Bonnet was recaptured after escaping imprisonment in Charleston.

The oppressive summer heat of Charleston and fear of yellow fever drove many early residents to stay on Sullivan's Island during the summer months. Building codes were strict, as was the law. According to *Island of History* by Suzanne Smith Miles, "lots were appropriated by building a dwelling house only—no mere shed or lean-to—and restricted to one dwelling on each one-half acre lot." All male residents between the ages of eighteen and sixty were required to patrol the island one night a week to enforce all laws, such as obeying horse and buggy speed limits and not

Fort Moultrie. Terrance Zepke

working on the Sabbath. Mail was delivered by a mail boat, which also carried fare-paying passengers.

By around 1850, the island village, Moultrieville was renowned as one of the best resorts in America. The Moultrie House, costing over $32,000, opened that summer and offered many amenities, ranging from billiard tables for the men to a spacious bath room for the women. Horse-pulled rail cars brought guests from the boat landing to the house entrance. Sadly, the luxurious hotel was destroyed during the Civil War. A lab for studying marine flora and fauna was established on the island in the early 1850s by scientist and physician Louis Agassiz, who also taught at the Medical College in Charleston.

By 1941, a school and some businesses had been established and twenty-five residents permanently resided on the island. Nowadays, the island has many visitors and residents year-round. The island's rich history can be seen by taking a self-paced tour through Ft. Moultrie and looking at former World War II bunkers, many of which are now underground dwellings. It is one of the few public beaches remaining uncluttered by huge hotel and condominium complexes.

TOURS & ATTRACTIONS
Ft. Sumter National Monument, located on an island in the Charleston Harbor, is dedicated to where the first shots of the Civil War were fired at Ft. Sumter from Ft. Johnson on April 12, 1861. Boat tours to the monument depart from Charleston's marina and Patriots Point

❧ ❧ ❧

Civil War has at last begun. A terrible fight is at this moment going on between Ft. Sumter and the fortification by which it is surrounded.

. . . at twenty-seven minutes past four o'clock this morning, Ft. Moultrie began the bombardment by firing two guns. To these Major Anderson replied with three of his barbette guns, after which the batteries on Mt. Pleasant, Cummings Point, and the Floating Battery, opened a brisk fire of shot and shell.

Breaches [in Ft. Sumter], to all appearance, are being made in the several sides exposed to fire. Portions of the guns there mounted have been shot away. It is not improbable that the fort will be carried by storm.

The soldiers are perfectly reckless of their lives, and at every shot jump upon the ramparts, observe the effect, and then jump down, cheering.

The excitement of the community is indescribable. With the very first boom of the gun thousands rushed from their beds to the harbor front, and all day every available place has been thronged by ladies and gentlemen, viewing the solemn spectacle through their glasses. Most of these have relatives in several fortifications, and many a tearful eye attested to the anxious affection of the mother, wife, and sister, but not a murmur came from a single individual.

The spirit of patriotism is as sincere as it is universal. Five thousand ladies stand ready to respond to any sacrifice that may be required of them.

New York Herald (April 13, 1861)

❧ ❧ ❧

Maritime Museum in Mt. Pleasant. The site is open daily except for Christmas. There is also a museum and gift shop. Hours of operation vary. (843) 883-3123. $.

SpiritLine Charters is the sole authorized concessionaire of the National Park Service so they it's the only boat tour that stops at Ft. Sumter. (843) 722-2628 and http://www.spritlinecruises.com. $.

Ft. Moultrie, on the northwest tip of the island, is the site of the first clear victory of the American Revolutionary War. The one-and-a-half-acre-fort you see today is actually the third Ft. Moultrie. Built in 1809 as a sea-coast defense, the restored fort has a visitors center and an interpretive

This Sullivan's Island house is an example of the new architectural style hurricane-proof dwelling. Terrance Zepke

trail that chronicles US history from the American Revolution to World War II. This fort served as a crucial harbor defense for over 171 years until it was deactivated in 1947. Ft. Moultrie became a National Park Site in 1961. Open daily. 1214 Middle Street. www.nps.gov. $.

Sullivan's Island Lighthouse, located on the north side of the Charleston Harbor near Ft. Moultrie, was built in 1962. The 163-foot beacon has the potential to be one of the most powerful lights in the world. The tower is constructed with unusual triangular aluminum paneling to best protect it against hurricanes. The lighthouse is part of the Coast Guard compound and is not open to the public, but it can easily be seen through the chain link fence and gate. Free.

ACTIVITIES

Island amenities include a public basketball court, exceptional fishing at Breach Inlet, swimming (except at Breach Inlet), and boating. Golf carts, beach chairs and umbrellas, kayaks, bicycles, and boats can be rented through Island Realty. They can also arrange parasailing, jet skiing, wave runners, and guided nature outings. 1304 Palm Boulevard, Isle of Palms. (800) 476-0400, (843) 886-8144, rentals info@islandrealty.com, and http://www.islandrealty.com.

NATURE & WILDLIFE

During my last visit to the island, I was standing on the dunes near the lighthouse and saw a large school of dolphins. I'm also told there are

❦ ❦ ❦

It [Sullivan's Island] consists of little else than the sea sand, and is about three miles. Its breadth at no point exceeds a quarter of a mile. It is separated from the main land by a scarcely perceptible creek, oozing its way through a wilderness of reeds and slime, a favorite resort of the marsh-hen. The vegetation, as might be supposed, is scant, or at least dwarfish. No trees of any magnitude are to be seen. Near the western extremity, where Ft. Moultrie stands, and where are some miserable frame buildings, tenanted during summer, by the fugitives from Charleston dust and fever, may be found, indeed, the bristly palmetto; but the whole island, with the exception of this western point, and a line of hard, white beach on the seacoast, is covered with a dense undergrowth of sweet myrtle, so much prized by the horticulturists of England. The shrub here often attains the height of 15 or 20 feet and forms an almost impenetrable coppice, burthening the air with its fragrance.

A description of Sullivan's Island from Edgar Allan Poe's *The Gold Bug,* 1843

❦ ❦ ❦

good shelling and bird-watching.

ENTERTAINMENT & NIGHTLIFE

Nightlife is restricted to what the local bars and restaurants offer.

Most of them provide music seasonally. **Dunleavy's Pub** is a lively place that serves spirits and food. (843) 883-9646.

ACCOMMODATIONS

Island Realty has villas, condos, and houses available for rent on Sullivan's Island and Isle of Palms. They also offer golf packages. 1304 Palm Boulevard, Isle of Palms. (800) 476-0400, (843) 886-8144, rentals info@islandrealty.com, and www.islandrealty.com.

RESTAURANTS

Most of the eating establishments, such as Bert's, Atlanticville, Saltwater Grille, and Station 22, are clustered on Middle Street and have a casual atmosphere and dress code. Tourist season runs Easter through Labor Day, and most restaurants have limited hours of operation in the off-season.

ANNUAL EVENTS
New Year Polar Swim (January).
Carolina Day (June).
Sullivan's Island Taste of the Islands (May).

NEARBY POINTS OF INTEREST
Charleston is 8 miles west of Sullivan's Island.

H. L. Hunley, the nation's first submarine, launched a successful assault on the *USS Housatonic* on February 17, 1864. Even though it was a victory for the Confederates, the ship sank afterwards and all nine men aboard died. The sub was raised near Sullivan's Island in 2000 and is on limited display in Charleston. Scientists are hoping the wreck will provide evidence to finally determine why the sub sank. From downtown Charleston, take I-26 West to the Spruill Avenue exit. Take a left onto Spruill Avenue and then a right onto McMillan Avenue. Warren Lasch Conservation Center (the former Charleston Naval Base), 1250 Supply Street, Building 255, North Charleston, SC 29405. (843) 723-9797 (Hunley hotline), (866) 866-9938 (ticket sales), and www.hunley.org. $.

Coastal Expeditions offers kayaking adventures along scenic waterways behind the island. They also rent kayaks and offer instruction. Shem Creek Maritime Center, 514-B Mill Street, Mt. Pleasant, SC 29464. (843) 884-7684 and www.coastalexpeditions.com.

TOURISM INFORMATION
Charleston Area Convention & Visitors Bureau. PO Box 975, Charleston, SC 29402. (800) 868-8118 and www.charlestoncvb.com.

Mt. Pleasant Visitors Centers. 100 Ann Edwards Lane or inside the Hess Station at the intersection of Highway 17 North and McGrath Darby Boulevard. (843) 849-6154, (843) 849-6479, and http://www.townofmountpleasant.com.

DIRECTIONS & ACCESSIBILITY
The island, 8 miles east of Charleston, is open to the public and there are two ways to access it. Both routes originate at Mt. Pleasant. Take US 17 or I-526 to SC 703 through Mt. Pleasant and across Ben Sawyer Bridge to Sullivan's Island. Or take the IOP Connector from Mt. Pleasant onto Isle of Palms and then cross Breach Inlet Bridge over to Sullivan's Island.

JAMES ISLAND
(FORMERLY BOONE'S ISLAND)

Population: 33,871

The first inhabitants of this island were probably the Cusabo Indians. In 1671, the state's second settlement, James Towne (also called New Towne), was established on the island and named after King James II.

The first shots of the Civil War were fired from Ft. Johnson on James Island to Ft. Sumter on April 12, 1861. Several plantations were built on the island during the 1800s, such as the McLeod Plantation. During its heyday, it was one of the biggest cotton plantations in the South. It was used as a hospital and officers' quarters by both Union and Confederate troops. Sadly, most of these plantations were eradicated during the War Between the States. Planters trying to avoid malaria, fled their plantations every summer for safe havens, such as Riversville. This village was later renamed Secessionville because older residents of James Island accused younger planters of trying to secede from their community.

This headland was used by the Confederates for defending the island. Protecting James Island was considered crucial in protecting Charleston from the Federals. For that reason, Ft. Lamar was set up on the upper part of this peninsula. Several island homes were destroyed so that soldiers could use the building materials for their own purposes. The two remaining homes, Secessionville Manor and Seabrook-Freer House, were used as a hospital and headquarters, respectively. Union soldiers lost a battle against the Confederates at Secessionville, which ended an impending offensive against Charleston.

After the war, the James Island Agricultural Society was founded by island planters who felt they needed to join together in order to thrive. They recorded everything, including what was planted, when it was planted, what kind of fertilizer was used, and how much was harvested. This gave the members valuable information about which growing methods worked and which didn't. In the beginning, membership was restricted to island residents, but so many planters from other areas wanted to join that this membership requirement was waived. Despite the best efforts of the agricultural society, the late 1800s were bad times for planters. Natural disasters wiped out crop after crop. What must surely have been perceived as a miracle was the invention of a disease-resistant cotton seed by E. L. Rivers in July 1900. The accomplishment is documented by the Department of Agriculture. Prosperous times returned to James Island until the boll weevil assault in 1919, which ended cotton growing statewide.

Agriculture remains vital to the island, but has changed to dairy and

A roadside stand offering "Sweet Grass Baskets". Terrance Zepke

produce. The James Island Agricultural Society still exists and meets every year on July 4th. Most tourists do not spend significant time here but pass through James Island en route to beach communities such as Kiawah and Folly Islands.

TOURS & ATTRACTIONS

There's not much of historic significance on the island except for a few old homes and churches, such as the **James Island Presbyterian Church, McLeod Plantation** (now a bed and breakfast), and **Marshlands Plantation,** which was built on the Cooper River by John Ball (circa 1810), later used by Charleston Naval Base, and now owned by the College of Charleston.

Little remains of **Ft. Johnson**. The land is now owned by the College of Charleston and the South Carolina Wildlife Commission. Both operate Marine Research Labs at the site where Union Major Robert Anderson surrendered to Confederate General Beauregard. Marshlands Plantation has been relocated to this site.

ACTIVITIES

James Island County Park offers bicycle, kayak, and pedal boat rentals, a climbing wall, playgrounds, and walking and biking trails. Fishing is permitted in the park's freshwater lakes. There is also a saltwater crabbing dock. The snack bar is open seasonally. (843) 795-PARK, (843) 795-7275, jicpcg@bellsouth.net, and http://www.ccprc.com. $.

Charleston Municipal Golf Course is open to the public. 2110 Maybank Highway. (843) 795-6517.

Public boat ramps include Riverland Terrace at Plymouth Landing, Battery Island (Sol Legare), and Wappoo Cut.

Splash Zone family water park, which has two 200-foot slides, a 500-foot lazy river with adventure channel, leisure pool, and Caribbean structure "with interactive play elements." The water park is adjacent to the James Island Country Park Campground, and admission fees are reduced for campers. Open May through Labor Day, weekends only in May and late August.

Sea Island Tours by Sites & Insights Tours provides two-hour tours to James Island and Johns Island and includes stops at Angel Oak, plantations, war sites, and island folklore sites. Tours of other islands can be arranged. Tours depart daily from Charleston's Visitor Center. PO Box 21346, Charleston, SC 29412. (843) 762-0051 and www.sitesandinsightstours.com.

NATURE & WILDLIFE

James Island County Park is a 643-acre park that includes 10 acres of open meadows and 16 acres of lakes. It is supervised by Charleston County Park & Recreation Commission. 871 Riverland Drive, Charleston, SC 29412. (843) 795-PARK, (843) 795-7275, jicpcg@bellsouth.net, and http://www.ccprc.com. $.

ACCOMMODATIONS

McLeod Plantation. This antebellum mansion is in excellent condition, and the grounds contain barns, stables, a gin house, and slave quarters. Reservations are required. 325 Country Club Drive. (843) 723-1623.

Harborview is a small bed and breakfast on 541 Harborview Circle, James Island. (843) 762-4466.

James Island County Park has ten vacation cottages that overlook Stono River marsh. Each furnished cottage has a kitchen, a television, and sleeps up to eight people. Nightly or weekly rates are available. Discounts for Charleston County residents. (800) 743-PARK, (800) 743-7275, and (843) 795-9884.

CAMPGROUNDS

James Island County Park has a full-service campground with tent sites and camper hook-ups, ceramic bathhouses, an activity center, a laundry, grills and fire-rings, and shuttle service to downtown Charleston, Folly Beach County Park, and Folly Beach Fishing Pier. Leashed pets are permitted. Reservations are recommended. (800) 743-PARK, (800) 743-7275, and (843) 795-9884.

RESTAURANTS

The best restaurant on the island is probably **Maybank's**. It has received great write-ups in many newspapers and magazines, including *Charleston Post & Courier* and *Bon Appetit*. Vegetarian selections are available, along with an extensive wine list. Open for dinner only; closed on Mondays. Dress is resort casual. 1978 Maybank Highway. (843) 795-2125.

Stono Café features Mediterranean, low-country cuisine, and vegetarian selections. Open for lunch, dinner, and Sunday brunch. Closed on Mondays. Casual dress. 1956 Maybank Highway. (843) 762-4478.

Charleston Crab House serves lunch and dinner daily. Menu items range from shrimp and grits to lobster tails. At the Wappoo Creek Bridge at the intersection of Highways 171 and 700. (843) 795-1963.

ANNUAL EVENTS

Summer Entertainment Series (June).

Festival Hispano (September).

Holiday Festival of Lights (November-December) offers a 3-mile driving tour featuring 125 displays that total one million lights. There are carousel rides, a gingerbread house competition, marshmallow roasts, train rides, an enchanted forest walking trail, photos with Santa, gift shops (including Santa's Sweet Shoppe), musical concerts, and more. James Island County Park. (843) 795-PARK, (843) 795-7275, (843) 762-2172.

Holiday Festival of Lights Fun Run and Walk (November) is a sneak preview 5K run or 2-mile walk that is held the day before the festival opens to the public. (843) 795-4FUN.

NEARBY POINTS OF INTEREST

The pier and boardwalk at **Folly Beach**.

Angel Oak at Johns Island.

TOURISM INFORMATION

Charleston Area Convention & Visitors Bureau. PO Box 975, Charleston, SC 29402. (800) 868-8118 and www.charlestoncvb.com.

DIRECTIONS & ACCESSIBILITY

Highway 30 permits traffic directly onto the island. From downtown Charleston, take Highway 30. From Johns Island, take Highway 700. Coming from West Ashley, take Highway 171. All these highways lead to Folly Road and the heart of James Island.

☞ FOLLY, MORRIS, AND BLACK ISLANDS

Population: 1,708

Folly Beach is a six-mile-long island just south of James Island. Cusabo Indians frequented the island until the 17th century. More than 22,000 Union troops occupied Morris and Folly Islands during the summer of 1863. Bombing practice was conducted on Folly during World War II. In the early 1900s, families began building homes on the island. The town was incorporated in 1936 and by the following year, it was a happening place to be. Tolls were collected for those wishing to come to Folly Beach, where dances, contests, and concerts were often held.

George Gershwin wrote part of *Porgy and Bess* while staying on the island one summer, but he wasn't the only famous entertainer to visit. When the Folly Beach's Atlantic Boardwalk was built, Guy Lombardo, Tommy Dorsey, and the Ink Spots all played there. Fire demolished the boardwalk in the mid-1950s, but it was rebuilt in 1960 and called Ocean Plaza. Sadly, another fire occurred in 1977.

Today, the Holiday Inn Oceanfront Resort and mammoth Edwin Taylor Fishing Pier occupy the space where the boardwalk once stood. Numerous tourists flock to Folly Beach every summer because of its pristine beach and convenient location near Charleston and Sullivan's Island.

Folly Beach Pier is ideal for strolling and fishing. Terrance Zepke

Morris Island Lighthouse showing keeper's house, equipment shed, and retaining wall. Courtesy National Archives

TOURS & ATTRACTIONS

The centerpiece of the island and beach is the **Edwin S. Taylor Fishing Pier**. This 25-foot pier sits 23 feet above sea level and juts out 1,045 feet into the ocean. The crowning glory of this grand pier is its 7,500-foot diamond shaped platform, which has a 1,400-foot covered shelter. The portion of the pier that presides over the beach is 10,000 square feet of souvenir and tackle shops, restaurants, and restrooms. No pets are allowed. There is no fee to access the pier but there is a fee to park in the lot. 101 East Arctic, Folly Beach, SC 29439. (843) 588-FISH.

On the western end of Folly, visitors can glimpse the 161-foot historic **Morris Island Lighthouse**. At one time, this was a four-mile island that separated Folly Island and Sullivan's Island. Just before the Civil War, Confederates stationed on Morris Island attacked a Union supply ship en route to Ft. Sumter. Union troops assaulted Morris Island in 1863 because the island was significant to blockade runners during the Civil War.

Morris was previously three distinct islands called Middle Bay, Morrison, and Cummings Point. (Middle Bay was near Folly, Morrison was in the middle, and Cummings Point overlooked the Charleston Harbor entrance.) The shifting channel required that jetties be built to save

Sailing around Folly Island. Terrance Zepke

Charleston Harbor. The jetties were completed in 1889 and caused erosion damage to Morris Island. Due to the erosion and the structural cracks caused by bombing practice during World War II, the Coast Guard decided to automate the lighthouse in 1938. They relocated the keepers and moved or destroyed all the buildings so that tides wouldn't carry them out to sea. Since that time, the entire island has been lost to erosion. The Morris Island Lighthouse seen today is actually the third. The original was built by order of England's King George III in 1767, and the last one was erected in 1876.

When Sullivan's Island Lighthouse was built, the old Morris Island Lighthouse was almost destroyed. Diligent local residents saved the light. The Coast Guard put an underground steel wall around the tower to protect it from further erosion damage. Today, the abandoned beacon serves as a daytime visual marker. It has become its own island in the Atlantic, with bits of its foundation flaking off and sliding into the water. The stairs are rusted but intact. Window panes are missing from storm damage, and vandals have removed the skylights. The iron and stonework in the lantern gallery and around the windows can still be seen. The lighthouse has endured just about every form of damage Mother Nature could throw at it, including earthquakes, hurricanes, and erosion. Residents would like to see something done with the beacon, but the US Lighthouse Society does not support saving it. And, since there is no land around the beacon, there is not much that can be done to make it accessible to tourists.

To get to the beacon, turn left onto East Ashley Street at the last stoplight before the oceanfront Holiday Inn. Follow this road until it comes to an end. There is a parking area on the right a few houses back from the beach. Proceed on foot for about a half of a mile. The lighthouse can be seen about three hundred yards offshore. Use insect repellent as I have been attacked by sand fleas and mosquitoes!

ACTIVITIES

There is a **public beach with fishing** off the pier permitted. There is no charge to walk on the pier, but there is a fee for fishing and parking in the lot in front of the pier. Nearby McKevlin's Surf Shop fulfills most aquatic needs, stocking everything from boogie boards to surfboards. Picnic and beach supplies can be purchased at Bert's Market and Mr. John's Beach Store. Both are near the pier.

Folly Beach County Park is a beach access park with more than 4,000 square feet of ocean frontage. Dressing area, showers, a picnic area, and a snack bar are available. Lifeguards are on guard seasonally. 1010 West Ashley Road. (843) 588-2426 and (843) 762-2172. Free.

There is a **public boat ramp** at Folly River Landing. Folly Marina, 66 West 9th Extension. (843) 588-3059.

Reel Screamer Charters offers a two-hour boat trip that takes passengers right up to the Morris Island Lighthouse. It also goes through estuaries for optimum birding and dolphin-watching. It also guarantees the best shelling expeditions in South Carolina. 1027 Oceanview Road, Charleston, SC 29412. (888) 349-4465 and (843) 762-7190.

ENTERTAINMENT & NIGHTLIFE

Most restaurants, shops, and nightlife are near the pier, such as the **Holiday Inn Lounge, Planet Follywood,** and **Islander Shag Club**.

ACCOMMODATIONS

Holiday Inn on Folly Beach, next to the pier. 116 West Ashley Avenue. (843) 588-2191.

RESTAURANTS

The Folly Beach Crab Shack. 24 Center Street. (843) 588-2060.
Seashell Restaurant. 10 Center Street. (843) 588-9001.
The Pie House. 39 Center Street. (843) 588-0265.
Melt Homemade Ice Cream. 23 Center Street. (843) 588-0111.
Starfish Grille (at pier). 101 East Arctic Avenue. (843) 588-2518.

NEARBY POINTS OF INTEREST

Sullivan's Island.
Charleston Tea Plantation on Wadmalaw Island.

James Island County Park.
Angel Oak on Johns Island.

At the entrance to Charleston Harbor, in the shadow of Morris Island Lighthouse, lies **Black Island**. It contains 50 acres of high land and nearly 2,000 acres of marsh. The three finger-shaped isles that comprise Black Island were bought by John Ohlandt in the 1970s to ensure developers couldn't destroy his childhood paradise. Over the years, developers have offered him millions for the pristine island, but he signed a conservation easement with the Low Country Land Trust in 1991 to make sure the island remained unaltered. Low Country Land Trust is a nonprofit conservation group dedicated to saving South Carolina's coast. Indians once hunted and fished off the island and Union soldiers chopped down island pine trees to build Battery Wagner on Morris Island. Named after an early owner of the island, the island looks about the same as it did many, many years ago. The only development Ohlandt has done is to clear a small foot path that extends across the island. It is inhabited with rabbits, raccoons, hawks, ospreys, and horned owls.

TOURISM INFORMATION

Charleston Area Convention & Visitors Bureau. PO Box 975, Charleston, SC 29402. (800) 868-8118 and www.charlestoncvb.com.

DIRECTIONS & ACCESSIBILITY

Twenty minutes from Charleston. The only way onto the island is via SC 171. From James Island or Johns Island, follow Highway 700. Take a right onto SC 171 and cross the bridge into Folly. From Charleston, take I-526 to SC 171 and cross the bridge into Folly.

JOHNS ISLAND

Population: 3,513

Johns Island is 10 miles wide and 32 miles long, resembling a horseshoe. It is separated from Kiawah Island and Seabrook Island by the Kiawah River, from James Island and the mainland by Stono River, and

❧ ❧ ❧

*The following is an account of Johns Island in the 1920s written by
Septima Clark during the time she taught school on Johns Island and rented a room on a farm on Bohicket Road. From A Place called St. John's
Island: The Story of John's, Edisto, Wadmalaw, Edisto, Kiawah, and Seabrook
by Laylon Wayne Jordan.*

*I went over there [Johns Island] in 1916. I finished Avery Normal
Institute at the age of eighteen. I went over to John's Island to teach because
black girls couldn't teach in the city of Charleston because segregation was
at its height . . .*

*Transportation was really a problem. There were no bridges and we
had to go by boat. It took me nine hours to go from Charleston down to
the Promiseland School where I was working and land at that place called
Mullet Hall that Limehouse owns today. I would leave [Charleston] at
three o'clock in the afternoon in a little gasoline launch and arrive there
at twelve o'clock at night. If the tide was not high then I could not land
and I would have to wait in that little boat until the tide came up the next
morning. Then I'd get out there at Mullet Hall and go to that school. I
would come home only at the Thanksgiving period because boats only
came on Tuesday and Thursday and I would be teaching and I couldn't get
a boat. I could have somebody ride me about eighteen miles down the
island to what we called Limehouse Bridge. There I could get a train and
go into Charleston and I could go back the same way. I rode on an oxcart
to school everyday because I lived about a mile and a half from the
Promiseland School.*

*Living there was an extremely hazardous kind of a thing. Most of the
people living on John's Island at that time had very uncomfortable houses
which were sort of little shacks. Even the white planters papered their walls
with funny papers. You could sit in there and read the funny papers when
you went to have your claim signed. The [School] Trustees on the island
would sign the claim before you could get your money in Charleston.*

*I had a room up in the attic of a house with a lantern in the ceiling.
On Saturday night which was the great bathing night, I could bathe down-
stairs in the living room where the chimney was when all the people went
to bed. This was the kind of life we had over there.*

*The people were real funny about religion and when the teachers
went to church and didn't have anything to say, there were considered not
to be Christians. In the summer time if you sat on the porch with your
stockings off they considered you not a Christian. They declared that the
devil was going to get that teacher because you had bare legs sitting out
on the porch.*

The man who I was boarding with had a farm. He had a store and his wife took care of the people and fed them at dinner time. Nevertheless, they didn't see that they should buy pots. They cooked the tomato sauce and things right in the can. They had big wash pots that they used to cook the fish. I never worried about the kind of living we had although I had been reared in Charleston with a mother who was a free issue and had been reared in Haiti. She had a lot of cultural ideas from the English. She came over to John's Island one Sunday and it was hard for her to see how I was living.

We had very little water although we were surrounded by Bohicket Creek. Very few had wells and they were open surfaced wells and when it rained everything went into that well. There was not any safe water. On Saturday when you would have to bathe, you would have to catch the rain water usually. You would get a tub full of water and bathe yourself, your hair, and your clothes all in the same water. There were no outdoor privies so people just used the bushes.

The Promiseland School was made of logs and in between the cracks they had clay. There was a big chimney with openings in both sides because it was a two teacher school. The chimney would heat the people right around the front, and the children to the back, like the teacher, were frozen in the winter time. My feet really got so frozen that I had chilled veins and there were no doctors on the island at that time. We had to pass this Angel Oak Tree to go to Wadmalaw to Dr. Barnwell who was the only doctor for the five islands nearby. Of course the people practiced their voodoo and witch doctor things. They told me to heat a potato and put my heel in it which I did and I almost lost my heel. I had to go to Charleston to get something done for my feet.

There were 132 black children of school age down there. There were two teachers and I had from fourth to seventh grades. The other teacher had first through fourth grades. There were not too many large children until November when the harvest was over. From the last of November to the last part of February we had the big children and the little ones came too. We would let the little children bring the babies because their parents signed contracts to go into the fields. We had little pallets made of quilts on the floor where these babies slept while I was there. The children brought little buckets with grits and oysters in them for lunch.

My school was painted black with creosote put all over it. There weren't but three white children down in our section. They had a white teacher for that school and it was white-washed. They had a bucket with a dipper. We knew this because we went with the white teacher to the Trustee's house to get our claims signed. The Trustee's wife would always give us a jar of pickles or preserves because she knew we were living in a different culture than what we came from. If the man was eating his supper when we went down there, we had to stay out on the porch and wait regardless of weather until he finished eating.

❧ ❧ ❧

from Wadmalaw Island by Church and Bohicket Creeks. Limehouse Bridge connects Johns Island to Highway 17 and the mainland. Like Wadmalaw and Edisto, Johns Island was once part of the mainland before erosion separated the two land masses.

Jacob Waight, a Quaker, received one of the earliest land grants for Johns Island. Twelve thousand acres were issued to Waight in October 1675. Over the next ten years, Waight helped settle nearly two dozen other Quakers on the northwestern part of the island. By 1700, there were more than fifty Quakers at Johns Island. Quakerism was eventually abandoned by second and third generations.

Plantations were self-sufficient by necessity because there were no retail shops, blacksmiths, or carpenters nearby. (Charleston was a day's journey by horse and buggy.) There was one tavern (1770) at Haulover Cut, Johns Island, operated by Thomas Smith. Popular island drinks included wine, rum, beer, and cider, but the most sought after were sangrias and toddies, which were smooth blends of wine or rum, sugar, spices, and water. In 1789, the census reported six hundred whites, 4,660 slaves, and forty free blacks and mulattoes living in approximately two hundred homes in St. Johns Parish. The average price for a one thousand-acre plantation with one hundred slaves on Johns Island in 1860, was $17,075. The same plantation cost nearly three times that amount, about $44,000, on Edisto Island. Planters on Johns Island established a summer retreat, Legareville (circa 1838), which was similar to Edisto's Edingsville. Johns Island planters purchased land from Solomon Legare. By the 1850s, twenty-five families had summer homes at Legareville.

Over the years, there has been much controversy over whether the island is Johns Island or John's Island. Most believe the island is named after St. John, one of the twelve apostles. Others argue it was named after some of its early settlers, John Cowen, John Caulder Wilson, and John Walpole. Official deeds and documents dating back to the 1830s show Johns Island as the correct name. That's how most long-time residents believe it should be written, and even the *Charleston Post and Courier* now refers to it without the possessive apostrophe.

Locals used to have more to worry about. During the Revolutionary War, there were a couple of skirmishes on the island. Thomas Fenwick passed valuable information on to British General Augustine Prevost. The spy told General Prevost that some American colonists they were looking for were on Johns Island and the British used the information to capture the enemy. Despite reassurances they wouldn't be harmed if they surrendered peaceably, many Patriots were killed by the British. There was also a battle at Wappoo Cut. The British defeated the Patriots because reinforcement troops were delayed by low tide. During the Civil War, two skirmishes took place on Johns Island: the Battle of Haulover and the Battle of Waterloo.

Angel Oak, the oldest living tree east of the Mississippi. Terrance Zepke

While both boasted small victories for the Confederates, they did not have a major impact on the outcome of the war.

There's not much on the island to attract tourists. There is no beach nor significant entertainment or shopping, but Johns Island is en route to several beach communities and resorts, so it is developing slowly.

TOURS & ATTRACTIONS

Angel Oak is a live oak that is 65 feet tall with a circumference of 25.5 feet. It is over 1,400 years old and provides 17,000 square feet of shade. A land grant was given to Jacob Waight in 1717 for some plantations, including The Point, which is the site of the Angel Oak. In 1810, ownership passed to his fifth generation heir, Martha Waight, and her husband, Justus Angel. The spectacular tree was tended for many years by the Magnolia Garden Club before it was turned over to Charleston in 1991. It is the oldest living tree east of the Mississippi. There is a gift shop, picnic tables, and rest rooms at the site. It is open to the public and is located close to the intersection of Maybank Highway and Bohicket Road. 3688 Angel Oak Road. (843) 559-3496.

Johns Island Presbyterian Church (1719). The edifice of the church was built using bricks shipped from England for the foundation and pine and black-cypress for roof shingles. In the late 17th century, a Presbyterian missionary, Rev. Archibald Stobo, was returning from a failed trip to start a missionary in Georgia. The ship, filled with refugees, docked in Charleston.

✍ ✍ ✍

Malaria was often referred to as fever because fever was a major symptom of the illness. Malaria was not as dangerous as yellow fever, which was life threatening. Yellow fever first hit the low country in 1699. It is believed the cause, the anopheles mosquito, arrived on slave ships. Other serious concerns included typhus fever, scarlet fever, smallpox, and the common cold. Because doctors were few and far between, islanders relied on healers to supply folk remedies. This is also the reason why planters moved their families off the island plantations during summer months to places less mosquito-infested.

✍ ✍ ✍

Stobo and his wife disembarked to get provisions. Upon learning he was a pastor, the residents asked him to preach and he accepted. A terrible storm arose while he was in Charleston and destroyed the ship and all the passengers who remained aboard. The decision to stay in Charleston to preach that sermon saved the Stobos' lives. Rev. Stobo accepted a position at a church and stayed in Charleston for four years before leaving to start churches on area islands so that residents could have services closer to home rather than commuting to Charleston every week. Johns Island Presbyterian Church was one of several that he founded. Stobo established the parish in 1710, but this church wasn't built until 1719.

Robert Fenwick was the first of his family to come to America and he engaged in piracy in the waters around South Carolina and in the Caribbean. He arrived in South Carolina aboard the privateering vessel, *Loyal Jamaica*. His brother, John, also came to South Carolina, but as a planter. John Fenwick built **Fenwick Hall** around 1730, designing it to look like his family's home in England. Located on the banks of the Stono River, the plantation has an underground passageway that leads to the river, and an observation area on the roof. No one is certain whether this was built as a way to safeguard against Indian attacks or simply to allow his brother to come and go without anyone knowing the pirate had been there. Edward Fenwick inherited the house from his father and owned it when it was used by the British Army during the American Revolution. Reportedly, one of Sir Edward Fenwick's daughters fell in love with a plantation horse groomer, and the pair eloped. They were caught at Stono Ferry. He was hanged for stealing the horse they used to escape, and his bride was forced to witness his tragic death. Many say her spirit lingers at Fenwick Hall.

Sea Island Tours by Sites & Insights Tours provide two-hour tours to James Island and Johns Island, including stops at plantations, war sites, and the spectacular Angel Oak. Island folklore is also shared with participants. Tours of other islands can be arranged. Tours depart daily from Charleston's Visitor Center. PO Box 21346, Charleston, SC 29412. (843) 762-0051 and www.sitesandinsightstours.com.

A CTIVITIES
Hope Plantation and **Oak Point** are par 72 golf courses that are open to the public. 4255 Bohicket Road. (843) 768-7431.

There is a **public boat ramp** as soon as you cross the bridge onto Johns Island.

Stono Marina. 240 Maybank Highway. (843) 559-2307.

V ACATION   R ENTALS
Benchmark Dunes Properties. 3690 Bohicket Road, Suite 1-A, Johns Island, SC 29457. (800) 992-9666 and (843) 768-9800.

Charleston Resort Properties. 2 Beachwalker Drive, Johns Island, SC 29455. (800) 845-7368 and (843) 768-9800.

A NNUAL   E VENTS
Holiday of Lights Festival on James Island (December).

N EARBY   P OINTS   OF   I NTEREST
Charleston Tea Plantation on Wadmalaw Island.
Kiawah Island.

T OURISM   I NFORMATION
Charleston Area Convention & Visitors Bureau. PO Box 975, Charleston, SC 29402. (800) 868-8118 and www.charlestoncvb.com.

D IRECTIONS   &   A CCESSIBILITY
The island is public, so it is fully accessible. Head south on Highway 700 from the greater Charleston area and you can't miss it. You can also take Highway 17 South and follow the signs to the island.

☞ KIAWAH ISLAND

Population: 1, 017

This ten thousand-acre island is 11 miles long and nearly 3 miles wide. It is named after the Indian tribe who lived here until the 1600s. It has been spelled several different ways through the years, including Kyawha, Kiwaha, and Keyawah, but ended up as Kiawah (KEE-a-wah). Believed to have been discovered by the white man in 1666, the land was later deeded by the Lord Proprietors to George Raynor, who may have been a pirate or, at the very least, associated with buccaneers, including the legendary Captain Kidd. Raynor sold the island to John Stanyarne in 1739. Sixty-eight years later, he deeded it to his son-in-law, Arnoldus Vanderhorst, the seventh governor of South Carolina, who introduced cotton growing on Kiawah. George Gershwin came to the island in 1934 when he was doing research for his renowned opera, *Porgy and Bess*. He called it Kittewah in the opera. From 1772 to 1953, Kiawah Island was owned by Arnoldus Vanderhorst and his heirs. Locals called them the "Kings of Kiawah."

It was nearly two hundred years before the Vanderhorsts sold the island to C. C. Royal of Aiken, South Carolina, who bought it for fishing and hunting. Royal paid $50,000 for the land in 1950 and received $17.3 million when he sold it to the Kiawah Island Company Ltd. (a subsidiary of Kuwait Investment Company) in 1974. They sold it to Kiawah Island Associates fourteen years later for roughly six times the amount they paid for it ($105 million). It was the most expensive real estate deal in South Carolina history.

Most of the island is privately owned, with more than 3,300 property owners from forty-six states and twenty-one countries. Only four hundred home owners live in Kiawah year-round. Residents and visitors alike enjoy its championship golf courses, top-rated tennis courts, and 10 miles of beach.

TOURS & ATTRACTIONS
Bohicket Boat: Adventure & Tour Company offers many types of tours and cruises around Kiawah and Seabrook Islands. 1880 Andell Bluff Boulevard, Johns Island, SC 29455. (843) 768-7294 and www.bohicket-marina.com.

Vanderhorst Mansion, built in the 1700s, is a four-story plantation house that was occupied by Union troops during the Civil War. The house has not been restored and is not open to the public. Call the Kiawah Island Visitor Center for location and more information. (843) 768-5116.

Bicycling Kiawah Island Terrance Zepke

ACTIVITIES

The Straw Market is a galleria of fine gift and souvenir shops, clothing stores, and sports equipment outlets. There are also a couple of low-key restaurants that have menus featuring sandwich and salads.

General Store/Bike, Beach & Sport Shoppe sells food, fuel, and souvenirs and rents bikes. (843) 768-2121.

The Shops at the Kiawah Inn sells gifts and sundries. (843) 768-2121.

Night Heron Park at the East Beach Village, is a twenty-one-acre park with basketball courts, a playground, a game room, soccer fields, a volleyball net, a fishing lake, a pool, and a fitness trail. Choose from boogie boarding, surf kayaking, jeep safari, canoe exploration, bicycling (either on a guided ride or on your own), and shopping at the Straw Market. There are many organized activities, ranging from alligator talks to kayaking tours. For information on recreation programs, nature tours, and special events, contact Heron Park Center. (843) 768-6001.

Kamp Kiawah offers a variety of fun programs for kids aged three to eleven. Call the Kiawah Island Resort Program. (843) 768-6001 and (800) 654-2924.

Half-day, daily, or weekly bike and gear rentals are available at **West Beach Bike Shop**. (843) 768-6005 and at **Night Heron Bike Shop**. (843) 768-6006.

Beachwalker County Park, situated on prime real estate between the ocean and Bohicket River, is just outside the island gates and is open to the public. (843) 768-6005.

Kiawah Island Golf & Tennis Resort has two tennis complexes, the

❧ ❧ ❧

The Legend of Vanderhorst Mansion

This old manor house is haunted. Arnoldus Vanderhorst IV loved to hunt and used to have great hunting parties. Quash Stevens, Vanderhorst's trusted servant, was in charge of organizing and leading these hunts. During one of the outings, Vanderhorst was discovered by Quash lying face down in a ditch. It is believed he stumbled into the ditch and was shot with his own gun when it discharged during his tumble. Quash's death was very hard on him, and the loyal servant and friend took to sitting on the porch of the mansion sharing stories and reminiscing about Vanderhorst and the fun they'd had when they went hunting. Visitors have reported hearing a voice that is believed to be Quash telling one of his stories.

Another version of this story is that Arnoldus Vanderhorst, not his servant, haunts his former home. Quash stayed on to oversee his former master's plantation and he frequently visited the house and found Arnoldus sitting, smoking a pipe. Quash also claimed the two men exchanged dialogue and occasionally walked on the beach together.

❧ ❧ ❧

East Beach Tennis Club and West Beach Tennis Club, which have received numerous awards and recognition, including "Top 10 Greatest US Tennis Resorts" by *Tennis Magazine* and "Top 100 Resorts in the World" by *Racquet Magazine*. Golf and tennis lessons and clinics are available. It also boasts four championship golf courses:

The Ocean Course, a par 72 course that has hosted the Ryder Cup and World Cup of Golf, designed by Pete Dye.

Osprey Point, a par 72 course designed by Tom Fazio.

Turtle Point, a par 72 course designed by Jack Nicklas.

Cougar Point, a par 71 course designed by Gary Player.

Just outside the island gates is **Oak Point,** a Scottish-American style course, which has been ranked among the top fifty South Carolina courses by *Golf Week*. This par 72 course was designed by Clyde Johnston. 12 Kiawah Beach Drive, Kiawah Island, SC 29455. (800) 654-2924, (843) 768-2121 extension 4010, (843) 768-2121 extension 1721, and www.kiawahresort.com.

NATURE & WILDLIFE

Kiawah has 30 miles of biking and walking trails that permit visitors a chance to enjoy the island scenery. There are sixty-five ponds and lagoons on the island and two lookout towers and observation piers. Its maritime forest is the perfect setting for nature programs, which include biking tours, beach walks, slide shows, canoeing, and shrimping. Programs originate at Heron Nature Center, East Beach Village.

The island does have bobcats, but they are almost impossible to spot. Alligators and deer are plentiful, as are loggerhead turtles during nesting season. Kiawah is a bird-watcher's dream. There are approximately 190 species of birds, such as herons, woodpeckers, bald eagle, hawks, osprey, egrets, wood ibis, and brown pelicans.

The island is full of many different types of trees, including palmettos, myrtles, oaks, pines, yaupon, sassafras, and magnolia. Wildflowers and sea oats also decorate Kiawah, creating a perfect backdrop and inspiration for artists and photographers.

ACCOMMODATIONS

Kiawah Island Resort Inn. 12 Kiawah Beach Drive, Kiawah Island, SC 29455. (800) 654-2924 and (843) 768-2121.

VACATION RENTALS

Beachwalker Rentals/Kiawah Island Vacations. 3690 Bohicket Road, Suite 1-A, Johns Island, SC 29455. (800) 334-6308, (843) 768-1777, and www.Beachwalker.com.

Kiawah Island Great Beach Vacations. 2 Great Beach Center, Beachwalker Drive, Kiawah Island, SC 29455. (800) 845-3911, (843) 768-

Kiawah Island Inn Resort guests can enjoy bicycling, golf, swimming, and more. Terrance Zepke

Kiawah Island Courtesy Charleston Convention and Visitor's Bureau

2300, info@kiawah.com, and www.kiawah.com.

RESTAURANTS

Restaurants are open to all Kiawah Island guests, but most are not accessible to day visitors. For more information on these and other dining options, call the Kiawah Island Visitor Center. (843) 768-5116.

Kiawah Island Inn has The Atlantic Room, Charleston Bar, West Beach Café, and Sundancer Oceanside Bar & Grill, the only oceanside bar on the island. (843) 768-2768.

Kiawah Island Villa Resort has Village Bistro (843-768-2121) and Night Heron Poolside Grill (843-768-6001).

Kiawah Island Resort Club has The Ocean Course Grill (843-768-2121) and The Dining Room at Osprey Point (843-768-2777).

Heron Park Grille features Southern cuisine. (843) 768-6001.

Rosebank Farms Café features low country cuisine and fresh produce grown by the family that owns the restaurant. 843-738-1807.

FESTIVALS & ANNUAL EVENTS

Oyster Roasts are held seasonally at Bohicket Marina and Mingo Point.

Kiawah's Summerfest Series is a summerlong series of outdoor concerts and shows. (800) 845-3911.

Kiawah Island House Tour (November) is sponsored by the Charleston Symphony Orchestra League. This is a good way to see island homes and dine in restaurants that are normally off-limits. (843) 723-7528.

Kiawah Island Craft Show (November). Contact the Kiawah Island Town Hall Visitors Center for more information on any of these events.

(843) 768-5116.

NEARBY POINTS OF INTEREST
Angel Oak on Johns Island.
Charleston Tea Plantation on Wadmalaw Island.

TOURISM INFORMATION
Greater Charleston Visitors Bureau. PO Box 975, Charleston, SC 29402. (800) 774-0006 and www.charlestoncvb.com.
Kiawah Island Visitor Center & Town Hall. 22 Beachwalker Drive, Kiawah Island. (843) 768-5116.

DIRECTIONS & ACCESSIBILITY
Located south of Charleston. Take I-26 East, exit 212 to I-526 West to US 17 South to SC 171 to SC 700 (Maybank Highway). Follow the signs. The island is semi-private; there are some publicly accessible places, such as dining at the Kiawah Resort Inn or shopping at the Straw Market. The guard at the entrance gate will issue a day pass and map to these authorized areas. No motorcycles, campers, or motorhomes are permitted.

SEABROOK ISLAND

Population: 1,044

Seabrook is a private 2,200-acre island located east of Kiawah, west of Johns Island, and 23 miles from Charleston. Kiawah and Seabrook are one island, geologically speaking, separated only by an inlet called Cap'n Sams (after an English colonist).

King Charles II sent British sailor and explorer Lt. Colonel Robert Sandford to the area, called Jones Island, and he arrived on Seabrook in 1666. The Stono Indians sold the land in exchange for clothing and trinkets. The English bought it in 1684 and the island was used by British and Hessian troops during part of the American Revolution.

The first crops produced were indigo and rice, but eventually they were replaced by cotton. In 1753, the island was bought by Ebenezer

Simmons and renamed Simmons Island. The land was sold to William Seabrook of Edisto Island in 1816 and was used to grow cotton until the Civil War. Seabrook bought this island in the 1700s as a hunting retreat and built his home on it around 1750. His heirs sold it in 1863 and it was ultimately bought by Seabrook Island Resort in 1971.

During the war, the island was sold to William Gregg. Gregg tried to reintroduce cotton production after the war, but was unsuccessful. He rented the land to Charles Andell of New York, who wanted to build a school to educate freed slaves, but the plan was never fulfilled.

After Charles Andell's death, his brother William resumed cotton production on the island, and he is responsible for creating a premium grade cotton. Like everywhere else in the state, the boll weevil ended Seabrook cotton production. William Gregg's widow was forced to sell the island to a group of sportsmen who used it for hunting and fishing.

The Episcopal Diocese of South Carolina rented the land in 1939 for use as a summer camp, Camp St. Christopher, for underprivileged children. Nearly 1,408 acres were deeded to the church in 1951, most of which were sold by the diocese to developers. The camp, however, remains the Episcopal Church retreat on Seabrook.

In 1987, the town of Seabrook was established. This very private, residential community has 3 miles of beach, and no hotels or high-rise condominiums have been built on the island. Every resident recognizes the need to protect the island's natural resources. The Club at Seabrook Island's golf courses became South Carolina's first "Fully Certified Audubon Cooperative Sanctuary."

Only resort guests and residents are allowed access to this island. I contacted the Homeowners Association to get a day pass, but my request to look around Seabrook (either escorted or on my own) was denied. I also asked the Seabrook Resort if they would issue me a pass, but was told I had to be a paying guest or they couldn't admit me. Therefore, all the information on Seabrook comes from the Charleston Area Convention & Visitors Bureau, and the town of Seabrook website, as well as various brochures and publications.

ACTIVITIES

There is an isolated 3-mile beach. There are two championship golf courses (Crooked Oaks and Ocean Winds), Seabrook Racquet Club (ranked among the top fifty tennis resorts in the US), two swimming pools, a fitness center, a full-service marina, waterfront dining, and shopping. Sailboats, bicycles, and fishing gear are available for rent. The island boasts a full-service equestrian center, which offers rides and lessons, as well as horseback or pony island tours that include a beach ride.

In the summer, special children's activities are planned. The Kids'

A Seabrook Island sunset Courtesy Hilton Head Chamber of Commerce

Club provides swimming, arts and crafts, field trips, and golf and tennis clinics. There is also a playground. Teens may enjoy pool parties, volley-ball, basketball, billiards games, and scavenger hunts. Seabrook Resort offers events for the entire family, such as ice cream socials, movie nights, pizza parties, casino nights, and bingo. The hospitality center features video games and ping-pong.

At **Bohicket Marina**, visitors can rent motorboats, sailboats, and skiffs; hire deep sea fishing charters; go surf fishing; crab at the crabbing dock; and take relaxing sunset cruises. Parasailing and kayaking tours are also available.

Bohicket Boat: Adventure & Tours Company offers many types of tours and cruises around Kiawah and Seabrook Islands. 1880 Andell Bluff Boulevard, Johns Island, SC 29455. (843) 768-7294 and http://www.bohicketmarina.com.

NATURE & WILDLIFE
Alligators, loggerhead turtles, deer, palmetto trees, wildflowers, cacti, sea oats, and more than 150 bird species

ENTERTAINMENT & NIGHTLIFE
Privateer Restaurant has a lounge bar and dancing. Open nightly during the tourist season. Dress is resort casual. Reservations are suggested. Bohicket Marina Village. (843) 768-1290.

Sunset Lounge (also called the Bohicket Lounge) is located above the Privateer and has big-screen TVs and music.

ACCOMMODATIONS

Lodging and tour packages are available. Packages include the family package, the historic Charleston package, and the romantic escape package, which includes a wine and cheese picnic basket, a carriage tour of Charleston, a bottle of champagne, a Charleston Harbor Cruise, deluxe accommodations, and more.

Seabrook Resort has one- to three-bedroom villas. The Village Center, 1002 Landfall Way, Seabrook Island, SC 29455-6303. (800) 845-2233, (800) 845-2475, info@seabrook.com, and www.seabrookresort.com.

VACATION RENTALS

Great Beach Vacations has many one- to six-bedroom homes and villas available for rent. 1001 Landfall Way, Seabrook Island, SC 29455. (800) 845-2233 and (843) 768-0880.

Beachwalker has short and long-term rentals on Seabrook. (800) 334-6308 and www.Beachwalker.com.

RESTAURANTS

Privateer Restaurant offers seafood and steak. Open nightly during the tourist season. Bohicket Marina Village. (843) 768-1290.

The **Island House** has a very extensive wine cellar. Not open to the public.

Red Sky Grille. (843) 768-0183.

The **Club at Seabrook Island** is a convention facility complete with restaurant and lounge. (843) 768-2500.

ANNUAL EVENTS

Spring Art Show features local and international artists.
The Charleston Summer Classic (July).
Bohicket Invitational Billfish Tournament (June).

NEARBY POINTS OF INTEREST
Kiawah Island.
Angel Oak on Johns Island.

TOURISM INFORMATION
Charleston Area Convention & Visitors Bureau. PO Box 975, Charleston, SC 29402. (800) 868-8118 and www.charlestoncvb.com.

Town of Seabrook Island. 2001 Seabrook Island Road. (843) 768-9121 and www.townofseabrookisland.org.

DIRECTIONS & ACCESSIBILITY

The private island, 23 miles from Charleston, is accessible only to residents, resort guests, and those renting homes on the island. You must have a pass or be on the list at the guard gate. A thirty-five minute drive from Charleston Airport, take I-26 East, exit 212 to I-526 West (Mark Clark Expressway) to US 17 South to SC 171 to SC 700 (Maybank Highway). Follow the signs. Or take I-526 (towards Savannah) to the end of the expressway and then turn right onto Highway 17 South. Stay on 17 for 5 miles, then take a left onto Main Road. Stay on this road for 18 miles until it becomes Bohicket, which ends at Seabrook Island.

✍ WADMALAW AND YONGES ISLANDS

Population: 2,611

The first inhabitants of this island were probably Cusabo Indians, a collective term for ten tribes: Kiawahs, Ashepoos, Bohicketts, Edistos, Escamacus, and Stonos. At that time, the island was full of wolves, deer, cougars, snakes, wild boar, and alligators, as well as many species of birds. When the European settlers arrived, their philosophy of hunting and living off the land differed from that of the Indians. Eventually most of the Cusabos were captured and sold into slavery. By the early 1700s, few Indians remained in the area, except on Wadmalaw and Kiawah Islands. No one knows the origin of the name Wadmalaw, just that it is an Indian word, perhaps a phonetic pronunciation of the Bohickett language. Over the years, the word has been spelled many different ways: Wadmela, Wadmelaugh, Wadmelaw, Wadmilaw, Wadmolaw, Wadmoolaw, Waha, and Waheawah.

Bounded on the south and west by the North Edisto River, on the north by the Wadmalaw River, and on the east by Church and Bohicket creeks, this 10-mile-long and approximately 5-mile-wide island on the Intracoastal Waterway, totaling 43 square miles of land mass, is primarily agricultural.

According to Allen Mitchell's *Wadmalaw Island*, most African-American males on Wadmalaw are unwilling to work on the area farms because their ancestors were forced to work the same fields as slaves. They prefer fishing, shrimping, and crabbing to farming. Most harvesting of Wadmalaw crops, including peanuts, tomatoes, strawberries, and cucumbers, is done by Hispanics, who come up from Guatemala, Mexico, Texas, and Florida. These migratory Hispanic families stay approximately three months and then move on when the picking is completed. There are cottages for these workers to live in while on the island, but there has been an ongoing dilemma as to how best to serve the community while accommodating the many migrant workers. Several years ago, an Arizona land developer attempted to construct several hundred single-family and multi-family dwellings on Wadmalaw, but the local planning committee did not approve the idea. They were trying to preserve the island's way of life and permanent population.

In 1666, Robert Sandford, sailor, explorer, and former army officer, was commissioned by the Lords Proprietors of Carolina to find land well suited to agricultural pursuits. This was the sixth year of the reign of King Charles II of England. On June 23, Captain Sandford and his crew of seventeen navigated what is now North Edisto River and Bohicket Creek. Sandford claimed all this area, including Wadmalaw, in the name of the king of England and the Lords Proprietors. In 1669, four ships set sail from England with colonists en route to Carolina. It stopped in the British Isles and West Indies to pick up more colonists. The 148 colonists arrived in 1670 and settled on the west bank of the Ashley (Kiawah) River and later moved to what is now Charleston. They survived those first four years through the generosity of natives, who supplied them with beans and corn when their crops didn't produce.

Subsequently, a 496-acre island plantation, The Rocks, was bought by Benjamin Jenkins in 1771. Part of his acreage included a small marsh island that was later used as a summer retreat for Wadmalaw plantation owners. During the state's Sea Island cotton-producing heyday, the crop was cultivated on Wadmalaw. In 1890, planters organized the first sailing regatta at Rockville, less than a mile from the tea plantation. The annual event still exists today but has grown from one day to three days. Rice planters moved their families to nearby islands in the summertime. That is how villages, such as Edisto Island's Edingsville, James Island's Secessionville, Johns Island's Legaerville, and Wadmalaw Island's Rockville, came to exist. A good example of a planter summer home is the Michah Jenkins House (circa 1770) at Rockville, Wadmalaw. It has been a summer retreat, residence, tavern, ferry house, and school.

Another dwelling worth noting was transported to Wadmalaw by T. Ladson Webb around 1970. The Charleston insurance executive had a

Tea leaves grow at Wadmalaw-Charleston Tea Company. Terrance Zepke

summer home on Wadmalaw until it was destroyed by fire. So he bought a large, antebellum house on Johns Island and had it hauled by barge the 30-something miles to Wadmalaw. It took almost three months to accomplish moving and securing the home at Bohicket Creek.

This Charleston County island also claims North America's only tea producer, the Charleston Tea Plantation, which produces American Classic Tea. The first Wadmalaw tea plants were imported from India, China, Ceylon, and other tea-producing countries. The tea is machine-cut every thirteen days from May to October using a mechanical harvester designed by American Classic Tea's Mack Fleming. While there are other tea farms that use these types of machines, most plantations harvest the crop by hand. All processes, from growing to packaging, are done on the plantation. The plants are completely free from insecticides and fungicides. In fact, the superior tea has been consumed at White House gatherings beginning when South Carolina Senator Strom Thurmond introduced Nancy Reagan to the tea during the Reagan Administration. Since that time, American Classic Tea has been used at gatherings with visiting dignitaries and for other special occasions.

America's first ornamental tea plants were brought to Middleton Place, near Charleston, in 1799 by French botanist André Michaux. In 1888, Dr. Charles Shepherd, a biochemist at the Medical College of South Carolina, founded the Pinehurst Tea Farm near Summerville, using various plants imported from around the world, primarily China. He died in 1915 and the farm went out of business. In 1960 Lipton Tea Company took cuttings and planted them at Wadmalaw. This was an experimental station and did not produce commercially until Bill Hall and Mack Fleming took over. Hall is a third-generation English-trained tea taster. While he grew up in Canada, his father and grandfather are from England and that is where were he was sent to complete a four-year apprenticeship. Until recently, there were tea auctions every day in London. Prices were set according to how the tasters evaluated the tea. Hall told me he tested between eight hundred to one thousand cups a day, five days a week during his apprenticeship. And unless he wanted to consume that much tea, which he only did with especially good blends, he spit after sampling. This means he also spits eight hundred to one thousand times a day! Hall has thrown away all the tea leaves harvested on a given day if they do not meet his satisfaction. Fleming is a former manager of Lipton Tea and the only tea horticulturist in the US.

There is nothing glamorous about this tea plantation. In fact, it is not really a plantation, but rather a 127-acre working farm. Bill Hall says that tea farms elsewhere in the world are called estates but he and Fleming felt that was too pretentious and settled on plantation. The plantation affords a good look into the tea growing and harvesting process. As a devoted tea drinker, I consider it a worthwhile destination, especially considering it is the only working tea plantation in all of North America. American Classic Tea is shipped all over the United States by mail order and exported to Japan. They have several blends, such as raspberry-flavored, Governor Gray, and First Flush, which is only harvested during May from selected "Carolina hybrid" plants developed on the plantation.

ANNUAL EVENTS
Rockville/Sea Island Regatta (August).

NEARBY POINTS OF INTEREST
Angel Oak on Johns Island.
Rockville is a quaint waterfront village, with fifteen to twenty homes, that is less than one mile from the tea farm. It is worth a drive through if you are in the area.

Like Wadmalaw, **Yonges Island** only has one or two places of interest to tourists. The first town on the island was London, which later became New London, then Wiltown, and finally Willtown. It was attacked by Yamasee Indians in 1715. At that time, it only had about twenty homes and a fort on the island. Many planters came to reside here and affluent New Yorkers and Charlestonians came to hunt on the remote island. After the destructive boll weevil ended Sea Island cotton production, locals

---

❧ ❧ ❧

The Gullah believe strongly in signs and rituals and have passed these beliefs and traditions to their kin. The older residents on Wadmalaw still practice some of these rituals:

At the end of a funeral, small children were passed over the casket to prevent evil spirits from coming back to haunt them.

Never try on someone else's hat or let someone wear your hat.

Never let someone comb your hair.

Stomping your left foot is bad luck; stomping the right foot is good luck, and you should wish for something after doing so.

If your right hand itches, it means you will receive a letter; if your left hand itches, it means you will receive money. If your nose itches, someone will soon be visiting.

If a rooster crows at night, someone you know will die.

❧ ❧ ❧

---

turned to shrimp and oysters for their livelihood. Prospect Hill and Morris Plantation are all that remain from Yonges' heyday.

T O U R I S M   I N F O R M A T I O N
Greater Charleston Visitors Bureau. PO Box 975, Charleston, SC 29402. (800) 774-0006 and www.charlestoncvb.com.

D I R E C T I O N S   &   A C C E S S I B I L I T Y
Wadmalaw is roughly thirty minutes from Charleston. The island is linked to the mainland and completely accessible to the public. Take Highway 17 South to Highway 700 (Maybank Highway) at Rockville. There are no signs for Wadmalaw so follow the signs to Kiawah and Seabrook and then turn right onto Highway 700. Go through Wadmalaw to Rockville. The gated tea plantation is on the left at the end of Wadmalaw Island and is only denoted by a small roadside sign. A long, unpaved driveway leads up to the main building, which cannot be seen from the road. A few dozen rows of tea plants are all that can be seen from the gated entrance.

The plantation's hours of operation change frequently. It's best to call and inquire. When it is open to the public, visitors may buy souvenir boxes and tea-related products in its gift shop. Visitors may also watch a free film and take a scheduled tour of the facility that includes samples of iced or hot tea. Free mail order catalogs can be requested through their toll free number. 6617 Maybank Highway, Wadmalaw Island, SC 29487. (800) 443-5987 and (843) 559-0383.

✍ E D I S T O   I S L A N D

Permanent beach population: 900
Edisto Island: 2,500

Separated from the mainland by the North and South Edisto Rivers, this fifty-five-square-mile island in Colleton County is one of the oldest settlements in the state. It was home to the Edistow Indians over 4,000 years ago, but they sold it to the British for trinkets. No one knows what happened to the Edistows, but it is believed that they merged with other area tribes. In 1674, the island was purchased by the Earl of Shaftesbury and a land grant of 600 acres was subsequently given to Paul Grimball. Grimball, along with his wife and two daughters, became the first settlers on Edisto. Most of his former home was destroyed by Spanish pirates in 1686, but remains of the plantation can still be seen on the North Edisto River.

The first crop grown on the island was rice, but the water was too salty to produce a good crop. The island began growing indigo when the British paid crop bonuses; it was lucrative business until the American Revolution. In the late 1700s, Edisto became a big producer of Sea Island cotton.

Reportedly, it was never sold at market because the special cotton blend was so highly sought that French mills contracted it practically before the crop was planted. Those who produced the fine cotton were rewarded with great prosperity. The valuable crop was heavily relied on until the early 1900s when the destructive boll weevil ended cotton growing in South Carolina.

Islanders used to amuse themselves with fishing, all night dances at the military hall that started at 8 P.M. and ended at sunrise with breakfast at one of the participant's plantation homes, sailing races, horse racing, and annual lancing tournaments that included the men dressing like knights and a mid-day feast. The knights, astride their horses, rode full-speed across a 120-yard course and threw lances through rings. Each participant was allowed three chances to accomplish this. Each chance lasted less than eight seconds. A panel of judges declared the winner and then he chose his queen. She was crowned and officiated over the evening's festivities.

Christmas was a magical time on the island in the mid-1800s. From the week before Christmas through New Year's Day, all work stopped. The plantation owners enjoyed banquets, oyster roasts, dances, horse races, and hunts. The slaves were given fruits and sweets and had joyous musical services in their praise houses. Plantation doors sported beautiful fruit-filled wreaths and entrances held cedar trees decorated with taper candles, popcorn garlands, and colored paper loops.

Marquis de Lafayette, the French General of the American

Revolution, visited Edisto in 1825. A reception was given on his behalf by William Seabrook and his family. The Seabrook Mansion, part of Oak Island Plantation, was a US Army Headquarters during the War Between the States. It was used by regiments from Ohio, Massachusetts, and New Hampshire. These occupying troops claimed all recently harvested or soon to be harvested cotton crops as "spoils of war." Jenkins Mikell set fire to his storehouses rather than see his cotton go to the enemy. Colonel Joseph Jenkins of Brick House was the delegate from Edisto Island to the Secession Convention. During the 1860 proceedings in Charleston, Colonel Jenkins stood up and declared, "If South Carolina doesn't secede, Edisto Island will." According to *Tales of Edisto*, "The Island became a no-man's land. The fine old houses were left vacant with the furnishings intact. Animals were turned loose to forage for themselves." Union soldiers took over the lovely plantation homes on Edisto.

Near the end of the war, many slaves had joined up with General Sherman and his men on their famous march through Georgia. He was not able to provide for them and so issued Special War Order Number 15, which entitled him to take all sea islands. He left 10,000 sick and starving freedmen. He appointed the troops stationed on the island to be in charge of providing food and shelter for these former slaves. They were crammed into every dwelling on Edisto, and soon disease, especially smallpox, was rampant. Army emergency rations were distributed until supplies ran out.

Missionaries arrived to teach the freedmen how to read and write. Later, James Pierpont Blake, who was the grand-nephew of cotton gin inventor, Eli Whitney, became Superintendent of Schools on Edisto. Blake, along with two school teachers, drowned in St. Pierre's Creek on Christmas night, 1865. His grave can be seen at the Presbyterian Churchyard. The schools became integrated in 1925 and the Consolidated School later became a recreation center when a modern facility was built. Nearly every high school graduate in the late 1800s and early 1900s attended either Winthrop College or Clemson College.

During World War II, soldiers patrolled Edisto's beach looking for enemy submarines. None were spotted. Residents often invited the servicemen in for coffee.

Today, tourism and truck farming are the economic mainstays. This laid-back beach community is perfect for family vacations or anyone wanting to get away from it all. Those who are tired of gridlock traffic and overcrowded beaches, will appreciate Edisto most of all. Its more than 2 miles of clean, sandy beach is perfect for swimming, sunbathing, and shelling. Visitors may also delight in looking for Indian relics along the marsh, or exploring Indian Mound (also known as Spanish Mount) on the beach that was used as a burial ground and ceremonial site.

According to *Edisto: Sea Island Principality*, Edisto Beach was once called McConkey Beach because it was owned by John McConkey. According to a gravestone in Edisto Episcopal Church, he was cruelly murdered but the culprit was never caught.

Edisto's beach was first developed by a company from Sumter, South Carolina, and sponsored by Mr. Mitchie Seabrook and Mr. G. Washington Seabrook, (both former owners of the beach). Development began in the 1920s, but progressed slowly due to the Great Depression of the 1930s. Those who owned beach cottages were mostly Sumter residents and there was no electricity or access road. Days were spent fishing, crabbing, shrimping, and surf bathing (swimming). Because of its remoteness, during Prohibition a ring of rum runners operated out of one of the back bays of the big creek that runs behind the beach. In 1977, five young men from out of state were apprehended on the beach for smuggling marijuana in a small sailboat from Colombia, South America.

The State Park opened in the late 1930s when the state park system was granted land for a park on part of the beach. A road and club-house/bathhouse were built by the Civilian Conservation Corps. It became the place to be until severe storms in the 40s and 50s caused tremendous park damage. The clubhouse was swept into the sea during a big hurricane in 1940.

TOURS & ATTRACTIONS

The Interpretive Center will open within the next three years at Live Oak Boat Landing. It will feature nature outings, led by volunteers, that will include eagle walks at Donnelly Wildlife Management Area, Grove Plantation tours, and Otter Island beach sweeps. Contact the Edisto Beach State Park for more information. (843) 869-2756.

Edisto Beach State Park is a 1,255-acre park built by the Civilian Conservation Corps in the 1930s. This salt marsh and maritime forest has a nature trail and beach access that allows visitors a bird's-eye view of the park's wildlife and nature. For those interested in staying overnight, the park has five cabins by the marsh and campsites for rent. The park offers summer naturalist programs, such as marsh and nature walks, fossils and shells, and dolphins and sea life. 8377 State Cabin Road. (843) 869-2756, (843) 869-2156. Open daily. Take Highway 17 to Highway 174, 22 miles to the entrance of Edisto Beach. The park entrance is on the left as soon as you enter the town. $

Coastal Expeditions offers kayaking adventures in the state park, including an overnight stay in a treehouse. They also offer instruction and rent kayaks. Shem Creek Maritime Center, 514-B Mill Street, Mt. Pleasant, SC 29464. (843) 884-7684 and www.coastalexpeditions.com. $.

The Edisto Island Museum and gift shop is operated by the Edisto Island Historic Preservation Society and contains exhibits and memora-

Edisto Island Museum. Terrance Zepke

bilia pertaining to the island's history. Open Tuesdays, Thursdays, and Saturdays 1 P.M.-4 P.M. Groups are accommodated by special appointment. On Highway 174. (843) 869-1954. $.

The Edisto Island Serpentarium houses alligators, turtles, exotic snakes, and more. It offers programs daily and you may have your photo taken with a snake. Open 10 A.M.-6 P.M. daily, May through Labor Day, Saturdays from Labor Day to October and during the month of April. On Highway 174. (843) 869-1171. $.

Pon Pon Guides Unlimited offers boat tours. (843) 869-7929. $.

Island Tours and T'ings offers a two-and-a-half-hour van tour of a plantation, churches, and other points of interest. They guarantee "exclusive access to private properties." They also have a gift shop. Highway 174 near Steamboat Landing Road. (843) 869-1110. $

Visitors should stop to appreciate the beauty of **Trinity Episcopal** (1880) and **First Presbyterian** (1830) **Churches**. On Highway 174.

ACTIVITIES

Public beach access is available on every block and beach-friendly wheelchairs are available free of charge from the Edisto Fire Department. (843) 869-2505.

There are three public boat ramps: Steamboat, Dawho Landing, and Toogoodoo Landing. Contact the Chamber of Commerce of the US Fish and Wildlife Service for more information.

Bikes and gear may be rented from the following three businesses:

The Edisto Island Museum details the island's heritage. Terrance Zepke

Edisto Bike Rentals. (843) 869-4575.
Edisto Essentials. (843) 869-0951.
Island Bike Rentals. (843) 869-1321 and (843) 869-4444.
Edisto Beach Golf Club is located in Fairfield Ocean Ridge. Designed by Tom Jackson, the par 62, championship course was once ranked among the top twenty-five courses in the state by *Golf Illustrated*. The fourth hole was once the sight of a Confederate stronghold. This is a pubic course that is open year-round. (843) 869-1111.

Edisto Beach Racquet Club is located in Fairfield Ocean Ridge. Hourly rates or weekly rates are available, as well as junior and adult clinics. The club is open to the public. (843) 869-0661.

The **Edisto River Canoe & Kayak Trail** extends 60 miles along the Edisto River, said to be the "world's longest free-flowing black water stream." The river is lined with cypress, red maple, pine, tupelo, gum, and huge oak trees laced with Spanish moss. There are seven public boat landings along the river: Green Pond Church, Canadys Bridge, Stokes Bridge,

Mas Old Field, Good Hope, Long Creek, and T. W. Messervy. Restroom facilities are available at Colleton State Park and Givhan's Ferry State Park. Givhan's also has cabins for rent. Visitors may bring canoes or kayaks and enjoy the river on their own or take a guided river trips with the Edisto River Canoe & Kayak Trail Commission. PO Box 1763, Walterboro, SC 29488. (843) 549-5591 and (843) 549-9595.

Edisto Beach Marina is a public marina located at the mouth of Big Bay Creek in St. Helena Sound. (843) 869-3504.

Edisto Watersports & Tackle offers parasailing, fishing charters, and ACE Basin boat charters, as well as bait and tackle supplies and groceries. 3731 Docksite Road, Edisto Island, SC 29438. (843) 869-0663.

Capt'n Richard's ACE Basin Tours offers scenic boat tours of the ACE Basin. PO Box 31254, Charleston, SC 29417. (843) 766-9664 and www.theofficenet./acebasin.

Hat Cat Blue Fishing Charters. (843) 869-4152.

Mudslinger Charters offers boat tours and fishing. (843) 869-3446 and (843) 869-3320.

Cruise Edisto with Capt'n Gus Gusler. (843) 869-3499 and (843) 869-5005.

Edisto By Water with Capt'n Mich Hutto has fishing trips, boat tours, and sunset cruises. (843) 869-0663.

Lucky Strike Boat Tours with Capt'n Dillard. (843) 869-4107.

These companies offer fishing charters, parasailing, boat tours, and kayak, boat, and waverunner rentals:

Edisto Watersports and Tackle. (843) 869-0663.

Ugly Duckling Charters. (800) 303-1580.

Miss Marisa Aquatic Tours. (843) 869-0088 and (843) 869-1430.

NATURE & WILDLIFE

The best opportunity to spot wildlife is in the 11,019-acre **ACE Basin National Wildlife Refuge,** named for the first letter of each of the three rivers that drain the basin—Ashepoo, Combahee, and Edisto. In earlier times, this area was filled with rice plantations. Sadly, most were destroyed during the Civil War. Only three antebellum homes in the basin area survived. One of these, The Grove Plantation (1828), is now the headquarters for this wildlife refuge and is on the National Register of Historic Places. The refuge houses endangered and threatened species, including bald eagles, loggerhead turtles, and shortnose sturgeon. The most abundant wildlife is birds. Many birds pass through during migration or make their home here, including the peregrine falcon, wood stork, ruby-throated hummingbird, and bald eagle. Other wildlife include alligators, white-tailed deer, bobcats, river otters, and gray fox. Pets are not permitted. Designated hunting is permitted in accordance with refuge rules. PO Box 848, 8675 Willtown Road, Hollywood, SC 29449. (843) 889-3084.

According to the US Fish & Wildlife Service, which oversees the ACE Basin Wildlife Refuge, "**Sport fishing** is permitted in the tidal creeks and fresh water streams. Access to tidal waters by boat is permitted through-out the year." Open daily. From Charleston, take US 17 to SC 174. Go through Adams Run, turn right onto Willtown Road. Go 2 miles and turn left onto a dirt road. The refuge is 2 miles ahead. US Fish & Wildlife Service. (800) 344-WILD and www.fws.gov/~r4eao. Free.

ENTERTAINMENT & NIGHTLIFE
There's not much nightlife in this beach community except what is offered by the local bars and restaurants. There is live music seasonally at **Dockside and Coots**. There is also a video store for movie rentals and an arcade with games.

ACCOMMODATIONS
There are no hotels or motels, but there are cabins and campsites at **Edisto Beach State Park**. (843) 869-2756 and (843) 869-2156.

VACATION RENTALS
Atwood Agency. 495 Highway 174, Edisto Beach, SC 29438. (800) 846-0126, (843) 869-2151, and www.atwoodagency.com.

Prudential KAPP/Lyons Company. 440 Highway 174, Edisto Beach, SC 29438. (800) 945-9667, (843) 869-2516, and www.kapplyons.com.

Edisto Sales & Rentals. 1405 Palmetto Boulevard, Edisto Island, SC 29438. (800) 868-5398, (843) 869-2527, and www.edistorealty.com.

Lachiocotte & Harper Realty. 8117 Oyster Factory Road, Edisto Island, SC 29438. (800) 962-1930, (843) 869-1930, and www.edistore-alestate.com.

Fairfield Ocean Ridge offers vacationers upscale villas, tennis courts, and a championship golf course. 1 King Cotton Road. (800) 845-8500, (843) 869-2561, and www.fairfieldvacation.com.

RESTAURANTS
All restaurants have a casual atmosphere and dress code. Most of these establishments are closed or have limited hours of operation during the off-season. Tourist season runs from Easter through Labor Day. Call the Chamber of Commerce for assistance. (843) 869-3867.

If you have trouble finding a restaurant for lunch, or even if you don't, you might want to buy some snacks at the grocery store and enjoy a picnic on the beach or in Edisto Beach State Park.

Pavilion Restaurant & Coots Lounge. 101 Palmetto Boulevard. (843)

869-3061.

Old Post Office has been written up in *USA Today* and several other publications for the outstanding low country cuisine. Don't miss their shrimp and grits! Open Tuesday-Sunday for dinner only. 1442 Highway 174. (843) 869-2339.

Dockside is a restaurant and lounge featuring local seafood. 3730 Dock Site Road. (843) 869-2695.

Sunset Grille is owned by the owners of Old Post Office, but Sunset Grille offers a different menu. (843) 869-1010.

Sea Cow Eatery. 145 Jungle Road. (843) 869-3222.

Heron House specializes in prime rib and is located in Fairfield Resort, but is open to the public. 21 Fairway Drive. (843) 869-1112.

Gallery Café offers desserts, coffees, light breakfast, and lunch while you enjoy art. (843) 869-JAVA.

Buck's Pizza. 114 Jungle Road. (843) 869-5000.

Po-Pig's BBQ was recently written up in *The New York Times*. 2410 Highway 174. (843) 869-9003.

Fat Jack's Restaurant. 136 Jungle Road. (843) 869-5253.

Jungle Road Café offers seafood and steaks, as well as burgers and sandwiches. 108 Jungle Road. (843) 869-4400.

Edisto Beach Café. 102 Jungle Road. (843) 869-4001.

SHOPPING

There is a bookstore with local and regional books, two art galleries, a camping and beach supplies store, and several gift and souvenir shops on the island. You'll also see roadside stands filled with locally made products, such as sweetgrass baskets. If you do stop, you'll almost assuredly be rewarded with a demonstration.

ANNUAL EVENTS

Annual Island Tour of Historic Plantations and Churches (the second Saturday in October) features Windsor Plantation, Middleton Plantation, Prospect Hill, and more. Sponsored by the Edisto Island Historic Preservation Society. PO Box 393, Edisto Island, SC 29438. (843) 869-1954. $.

Governor's Cup Bill Fishing (May). Contact the Chamber of Commerce for more information. (843) 869-3867. $.

NEARBY POINTS OF INTEREST

Angel Oak on John's Island.

Charleston Tea Plantation on Wadmalaw Island.

Edisto Nature Trail is a mile-long trail, located right before Highway 17 South and the Walterboro exit (SC 64). It is on Highway 17 in

∅ ∅ ∅

According to Nell Graydon's *Tales of Edisto*, 1955, "Some of the medley of African voodoo brought to the Island by the slaves over a hundred and fifty years ago undoubtedly is still practiced by the Negroes in a small way. Many of the customs and beliefs have gone with the passing of the older generations, but all the Negroes are superstitious, especially concerning the dead. The Negroes paint their doors and shutters a bright blue to keep out evil spirits. It is said that in the early days they used the skimming from the indigo pots. *Sparits*, Negroes claims, are able to assume all kinds of shapes; after midnight the dead rise from their graves and walk in the form of goats, dogs, and other animals. It is almost impossible to get some of the Edisto Negroes to pass certain places after dark. Certain old women have the power to make love charms and to cast spells that cause sickness and sometimes death. Dried frogs, snakes, lizaes, and black cats are used to brew concoctions for various purposes."

The author demonstrates these beliefs by citing some examples, including a personal experience. Graydon once had a laundress named Toria who took ill. They tried various treatments but nothing worked. She offered to take Toria to a doctor in Charleston but the woman refused. "T'ain't no use, Missus," she said sadly, "I gwine see death. Beula, e done hab ole Riah f'row spell puntop me. Jist yestiddy top do'step uh fin' dried toad. T'ain't no use." Having heard of Mariah and her reputation for conjuring charms, Graydon went to the woman's cabin to ask her to leave Toria alone. She also gave her a bribe of two bags of tobacco and several small pieces of silver. She grinned and snatched the items, promising "Fuh sutt'n, Missus, Riah help Toria. Tell she attuh w'ile she be well. Riah suh so." The message was delivered to Toria and sure enough, the woman was soon well.

When Toria's husband, Bi'man, complained of chest pains, Toria begged Graydon to intercede again. A woman named Beulah had fallen in love with Bi'man but he had resisted her advances. The couple believed Beulah had gotten Mariah to cast a spell. Once more, Graydon rode down the sand road to Riah's cabin and took bribes—tobacco and groceries. The purpose of the visit had not yet been explained but the woman seemed to know already. After examining the goods, she pulled a corncob doll, which looked like a man, from an old chest. A string was wrapped tightly around the doll's chest and as the woman unwound the cord that smelled strongly like kerosene, she told Graydon to take the doll to Toria and to tell her to keep it and no *sparits* would ever harm her family. Although Nell Graydon had a hard time imagining how unraveling a string from a doll could cure someone, Bi'man's pains stopped almost immediately.

∅ ∅ ∅

Jacksonboro, southeast of Walterboro. Trail maps can be found at the start of the trail. Wildlife and nature include cypress swamp, deer, songbirds, owls, lizards, and more. (843) 871-5000.

According to Nell Graydon's *Tales of Edisto*, **Botany Bay** "was an adjunct to [the Jenkins Mikell] plantation, an island of wild oaks, palmettos, and cedar, a tropical jungle impenetrable twenty yards from the beach, five miles long and a half-mile wide, inhabited by deer, marsh tackeys (wild ponies which are believed to have been brought by Indians and to have drifted down from North Carolina Shakleford Banks, which are believed to have been brought there by Sir Walter Raleigh's colonists), wild hogs and half-wild cattle (hence the name Botany Bay). The beach was unsurpassed on the Atlantic coast and nearby tasty White-foot oysters could be found. They were named after a tribe of White-foot Indians, a subdivision of the Edistoes, who claimed and maintained their dominion over the territory in a hard fought battle."

Botany Island is on the ocean, just past Seabrook Island. It is comprised of approximately 200 acres, mostly beach. I have been told that about 40 years ago, a group of locals got together and bought the island for roughly $15,000. They later sold it for $65,000 or so. At that time, there was a fire truck, electricity, a caretaker, and one house on the island. Recently, the land was donated to the Nature Conservancy, except for about ten lots that were sold for development. It is not open to the public.

Edingsville was once a summer retreat for Edisto planters. There were over 60 houses on the island by 1820, including one owned by William Seabrook. Every house had flower and vegetable gardens, slave quarters, and carriage houses. The island was owned by the Edings family and lots were leased for $400 a year for ten years, with the right to renew leases. Summers were spent sailing, swimming, and enjoying afternoon teas and dances. In those days, disputes were sometimes settled with duels. These challenges were often completed at The Sands.

One such duel is chronicled in both *Edisto: A Sea Island Principality* and Jenkins Mikell's *Rumbling of the Chariot Wheels*. A duel was set up to solve an altercation between a Mr. Gilling and a Mr. Bailey. Gilling was as good a marksman as Bailey was a poor one. Reportedly, Bailey arrived with his second (required by dueling rules), his doctor, and a mattress for carrying his corpse back home. The seconds relayed the rules and everyone took his designated position. Paces were counted off and the two men turned to face each other. Overly confident, Gilling took his time aligning his shot while Bailey nervously fired off a couple of shots. Remarkably, one of the bullets hit his opponent and it was Gilling who went home on the mattress. Arthur Alfred Gilling was buried on February 12, 1839, in the Presbyterian churchyard.

According to Puckette's *Edisto: A Sea Island Principality,* Edingsville was jokingly nicknamed the "Riviera of the Low Country." There was a church, peach orchards, plum and fig trees, and cisterns for catching fresh water. A survey map done in July 1866 for J. E. Edings, shows 50 large beach lots of which 42 contained dwellings. A horrific hurricane wiped out most of the structures on the island in 1893. Pieces of pewter and china from these antebellum homes built on this seaside resort are still found occasionally by hunters, fishermen, and explorers.

According to legend and *Tales of Edisto*, the spirit of a stunning young woman, dressed in white, can be seen "when the moon is full and the north wind blows, making the waves dash angrily on the shore." She soon disappears into the surf. Apparently, there was a hurricane well over a hundred years ago that caused a shipwreck. As a result, a young girl was died and washed up on shore. A service was held and she was buried near one of the churches. What is believed to be her spirit has been seen by those aboard oyster boats and fishermen who come to the island because of excellent bass and trout fishing. Sadly, as what often happens to sea islands, Edingsville has eroded into little more than a sandbar and will ultimately be claimed by the sea.

Pine Island has a nice, white beach for boaters looking for a private sunning spot.

When it opens, the Interpretive Center will offer nature outings to **Otter Island**. Otter Island, protected by the South Carolina Department of Natural Resources, is open for camping November through April. Located off the southern tip of Edisto Island, Otter has great shelling. It has no amenities or resources but is beautiful. It is accessible only at high tide due to sandbars.

Cap'n Richard's **ACE Basin Tour** is a boat tour of the area's wildlife refuges. It covers the Combahee River area, which is one of the three rivers of the ACE Basin. It goes by old rice plantations and fields, and Cap'n Richard can identify all plants and animals and tells delightful stories that all ages can enjoy. A picnic lunch, complete with wildflowers picked during the cruise, is included. (843) 766-9664. $

TOURISM INFORMATION
Edisto Chamber of Commerce. PO Box 206, Edisto Island, SC 29438. (888) 333-2781, (843) 869-3867, and www.edistochamber.com.

DIRECTIONS & ACCESSIBILITY
Edisto is six hours from Atlanta, four hours from Charlotte, and about forty-five minutes from Charleston (50 miles southeast of Charleston). Take I-95 to exit 57. Then take SC 64 East to US 17 North. From US 17, take Highway 174 to Edisto Island (the road ends on the island). From downtown Charleston, take US 17 South to SC 174 and follow the signs.

BEAUFORT
ISLANDS

BEAUFORT

Population: 11,000

Beaufort County: 120,937

It's believed Beaufort was first inhabited 4,000 years ago by Archaic Indians. Europeans arrived in 1521 and for the next two hundred years, the French, Spanish, and English fought to call it their own. Meanwhile, Yamasee and Toscarora Indians also had conflicts over the land. In 1710, the Lords Proprietors granted the petition for a township, Port Royal, and in 1712, St. Helena was established. It is unknown exactly when Beaufort was founded, but by 1759 there were approximately thirty homes in Beaufort. Streets were named in honor of prominent people from England or their positions, such as King and Duke, and the town was named in honor of the second Duke of Beaufort, Henry Somerset.

By the Revolutionary War, Beaufort had a population of 4,000 and wasn't really affected by the war until 1779 when the British sent the *HMS Vigilant* to seize the town. General William Moultrie headed off British forces before they reached Beaufort, but the troops stationed at Ft. Lyttleton thought the enemy was going to win. So they destroyed the fort and that meant they were no longer able to protect Port Royal Island. The British took control of Beaufort, but only controlled the seaport for about three months before American troops, with the aid of the French, freed Beaufort. Skirmishes between the Tories and Whigs continued, and the town was left in a sad state by the end of the war.

Beaufort became home to many great plantations in the early 1800s when Sea Island cotton put the small port town on the map. Between 1790 and 1860, many planters got rich off Sea Island cotton. Beaufort was a prosperous city, and it showed. Beaufort College was built in 1795 as a

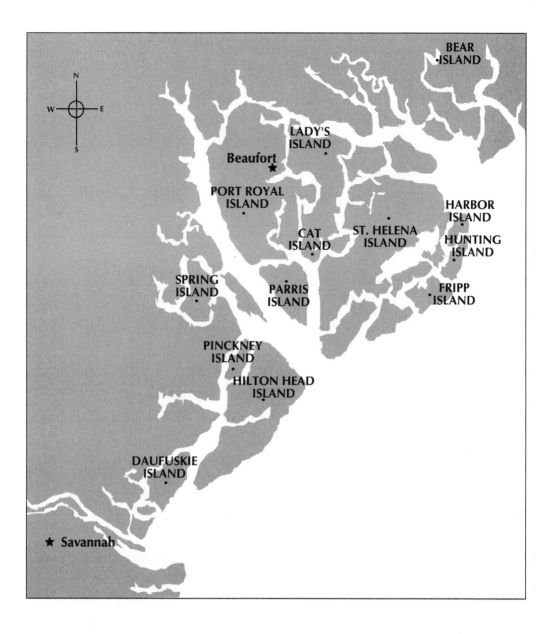

The Boardwalk. Greater Beaufort Chamber of Commerce

preparatory school for planters' sons, who would go on to complete their education at Yale, Harvard, or Princeton. Young women were taught by tutors and governesses. They learned skills such as ballroom dancing, music, and etiquette. Most attended a finishing school in Charleston. Streets were paved using oyster shells. Homes were large and elegant with columns and porches, drawing from several styles of architecture, such as Colonial, Georgian, and Spanish.

When the Civil War broke out, residents fled Beaufort, and Union troops used the abandoned homes as hospitals and headquarters. The seaport never regained the prosperity it had known before the War Between the States because an 1893 hurricane devastated Beaufort, then the boll weevil destroyed Sea Island cotton production across the state. Planters were forced to grow different, less lucrative, crops, such as vegetables and livestock feed. Today, seafood, lumber milling, USC-Beaufort, Parris Island USMC base, and tourism keep the area's economy strong. The city of Beaufort is only 3.67 square miles, but Beaufort County encompasses 587.3 square miles of land mass. Additionally, the county extends 30 miles along the Atlantic Ocean and includes sixty-seven major islands and hundreds of small islands.

There are many wonderful things to see in historic Beaufort such as this church. Greater Beaufort Chamber of Commerce

HISTORIC TOURS

The Visitor's Center has free maps that show the Historic District and describe each historic site. (800) 638-3525, (843) 524-3163, and www.beaufortsc.org.

The city's rich history is detailed in the **Beaufort Museum,** housed in the Beaufort Arsenal. In addition to collections pertaining to Beaufort and other areas of the low country, the arsenal itself exemplifies the city's past. In 1795, the South Carolina government authorized the construction of a "powder magazine and laboratory for the making of shot and explosives." The arsenal has served many purposes over the years, such as hosting women's auxiliary groups during both world wars. It is open 10 A.M.-4 P.M., Monday-Saturday, closed holidays. 713 Craven Street, Beaufort, SC 29901-1167. (843) 525-7077 and www.beaufortcitysc.com. $

Another great way to learn about Beaufort's history is by visiting the **John Mark Verdier House Museum**. The Federal-style home was built circa 1800 and is open to the public 10:30 A.M.-4 P.M., Monday-Saturday. 801 Bay Street. (843) 524-6334. $

The North Street Aquarium is open 10 A.M.-6 P.M., Thursday-Saturday and by appointment. 608 North Street. (843) 524-1559. $

Old Sheldon Church was burned by British troops during the

Revolutionary War, but the ruins still reveal its architectural style and lay-out. Shadowed by weeping willows, the ruins make a wonderful back-drop for special occasions. At the junction of Highway 21 and Highway 235, 1.7 miles north of the Highway 21 and Highway 17 junction near Garden City. Free.

WATER TOURS

ACE Basin Tours offers eco-tours aboard a pontoon boat. (888) 814-3129 and www.acebasintours.com. $

The Islander Steamship provides scenic Beaufort River boat tours. (843) 524-4000. $

Capt. Dick's Original Beaufort River Eco/Historical Cruises take up to six passengers on river cruises that explore nature, dolphins, former plantation homes, and more. (843) 524-4422. $

CARRIAGE TOURS

Carolina Buggy Tours. (843) 525-1300 and (843) 524-8600. $

Southurn Rose Buggy Tours. (843) 271-2130. $

VAN/BUS TOURS

The Point Historic Tours and Transportation. (843) 522-3576. $

Beaufort Tour Services. (843) 525-1300. $

Self-guided **All About Beaufort** driving tour. (843) 846-6847. $

WALKING TOURS

The Spirit of Old Beaufort offers guided walking tours, self-guided audio cassette tours, carriage, bus, and boat tours. 103 West Street Extension. (843) 525-0459. $.

Ghosts of the South is a candlelight walking tour through the Old Point Historic district. (843) 252-2586. $.

ACTIVITIES

Country Club of Beaufort is a par-72, Russell Breeden–designed, tournament-level golf course. Open to the public. Lady's Island at Pleasant Point Plantation. (843) 522-1605 and (800) 869-1617. $

Lowcountry Bicycles offers bicycle rentals. 904 Port Republic Street. (843) 524-9585. $

Deep sea fishing is offered aboard the **Seawolf**. Departs from Port Royal Landing Marina and also picks up passengers on Hilton Head Island. (843) 525-6664. $

Bay St. Outfitters provides Lowcountry inshore fishing charters. (843) 524-5250. $

Captain Eddies Fishing Charters offers a variety of options. (843) 838-3782. $

Carriage tours are a popular way to see Beaufort's historic district. Greater Beaufort Chamber of Commerce

NATURE & WILDLIFE

Nature lovers may opt to take a **Guided Marsh Walk** with the North Street Aquarium. (843) 524-1559. $

Go kayaking with **The Kayak Farm** at 1289 Sea Island Parkway, Highway 21 South, St. Helena Island. (843) 838-2008. $

The **Downtown Marina** offers boat rentals and charters. 1010 Bay Street. (843) 524-4422. $

ACE Basin Adventures offers kayaks, powerboats, and driving tours. Ashepoo River-Highway 17. (843) 844-2514 and www.acebasinadventures.com. $

ENTERTAINMENT & NIGHTLIFE

There aren't any nightclubs in Beaufort, but many restaurants, resorts, and hotels offer entertainment. See the Hilton Head Island section for more options.

ACCOMMODATIONS

Comfort Inn. (800) 423-8466 and (843) 525-9366.

Hampton Inn. (800) 426-7866 and (843) 986-0600.

Holiday Inn has lounge and restaurant. (800) 465-4329 and (843) 524-2144.

Red Carpet Inn. (800) 251-1961 and (843) 521-1121.

Best Western Sea Island Inn. (843) 555-2090.

A popular place to visit is the ruins of Old Sheldon Church. Greater Beaufort Chamber of Commerce

Best Inn. (800) BESTINN, (800) 237-8466, and (843) 524-3322.
Days Inn. (800) DAYSINN, (800) 329-7466, and (843) 726-8156.
Howard Johnson Express Inn. (800) 446-4656 and (843) 524-6020.
Sleep Inn. (800) SLEEPINN and (843) 522-3361.
Econo Lodge. (843) 521-1555, (800)-55-ECONO, and (800) 553-2666.

B E D   &   B R E A K F A S T   I N N S

Beaufort Inn is an elegantly decorated bed and breakfast with twelve guest rooms. It has been voted "Top Ten Inns in the Country" by American Historic Inns, partly in thanks to its resident gourmet chef. 809 Port Republic. (843) 521-9000 and www.beaufortinn.com.

Craven Street Inn has seven guest rooms room and a cottage. The special touches of this award-winning inn include room service, home-baked treats, fresh fruits, and juice each morning. 1103 Craven Street. (888) 522-0250, (843) 522-1668, and www.cravenstreetinn.com.

The Cuthbert House Inn is on the National Register of Historic Places. Truly beautiful and, like most things in Beaufort, on the water. 1203 Bay Street. (800) 327-9275, (843) 521-1315, and www.cuthbert-houseinn.com.

The Rhett House Inn, built in 1820 has seventeen guest rooms, free

bicycles, and provides full breakfast, afternoon tea, and hors d'oeuvres. 1009 Craven Street. (888) 480-9530, (843) 524-9030, and www.inn-book.com/rhett.html.

Two Suns Inn Bed & Breakfast claims to have "A Million Dollar Bayview" and is on Bay Street in the historic district. (843) 522-1122 and www.twosunsinn.com.

Old Point Inn has four guest rooms, a library, and gardens. (843) 524-3177.

VACATION RENTALS
Fred Kuhn Realty. (843) 524-8593.
Home Town Realty. (843) 522-0066.

RESTAURANTS
Magnolia Bakery Café specializes in homemade soups, breads, and desserts. They also serve salads, sandwiches, beer, wine, and espresso. Open Monday-Saturday. 703 Congress Street. (843) 524-1961.

John Cross Tavern was built in 1770 and is considered to be one of Beaufort's best historic landmarks. The menu includes Greek cuisine, steaks, and local seafood. They serve dinner only, but the tavern is open nightly until 11 P.M. 812 Bay Street. (843) 524-3993.

Ollie's By the Bay has riverfront dining featuring Angus beef, local seafood (including oysters shucked at the table!), pasta, and children's menu. 822 Bay Street. (843) 524-2500.

Emily's is an upscale restaurant at 906 Port Republic Street. (843) 522-1866.

Bistro 205 has been featured on the Food Network, in *Southern Living*, and has won the James Beard Award. It offers "casual dining in an art-infused surrounding." Lunch is served Tuesday-Saturday and dinner is served Monday-Saturday. There is an ethnic menu on Wednesday and live jazz on Fridays. 205 West Street. (843) 524-4994.

Plums is a local waterfront favorite that offers steaks, pasta, and seafood in a casual atmosphere. They have an extensive beer and wine selection. Lunch and dinner are served daily. 904-1/2 Bay Street, Waterfront Park. (843) 525-1946.

The Bank Waterfront Grill & Bar. (843) 522-8831.
Blackstone's Deli Café. (843) 524-4330.
Luther's Rare and Well Done. (843) 521-1888.
Hemingways Bistro, with weekend entertainment. (843) 521-4480.
Firehouse Books & Espresso Bar is a coffeehouse that sells books and gifts. It serves lunch daily, as well as homemade desserts (pastries are their specialty). 706 Craven Street. (843) 522-2665.

Shopping

Shoppers can find everything from art to clothing in the many quaint shops lining Bay Street.

Chocolate lovers won't want to miss **The Chocolate Tree**. If you're worried about the temptation, just watch them make the treats from outside the big storefront window. Open daily. 507 Carteret Street. (800) 524-7980 and (843) 524-7980.

Lowcountry specialty gifts can be found at **Bubba's By the Bay**. 900 Republic Street. (843) 524-3005.

Antique collectors may want to stop in at the **Collectors Antique Mall** on Ribaut Road. (843) 524-2751.

Festivals & Annual Events

Spring Tour of Homes (March).

A Taste of Beaufort (April).

Fall Festival of Houses & History (October). Historic Beaufort Foundation. (843) 524-6334 and www.historicbeaufort.org.

Shrimp Festival (October). Free but you must buy tickets for samples.

Parade of Homes (every other November).

Water Festival (July). This is a ten-day celebration complete with concerts, boat races, a decorated boat parade, talent competitions, a low-country supper, and more. www.waterfestival.com. Free.

A Night on the Town (December).

Festival of Trees (December).

Gullah Festival (May).

Nearby Points of Interest

Port Royal

Beaufort is on Port Royal Island, which also contains the town of Port Royal. Port Royal Island was discovered by the Spaniards in the 1500s, but no setttlement was established until the 1600s. The colony grew and became the town of Port Royal in 1874. The town prospered until the horrific hurricane of 1893, which wiped out crops and homes all over the area. In time, the island recovered and now this quaint island overlooking Beaufort River boasts more than 500 businesses.

There are many activities for visitors, especially shopping and dining. A thirty-minute walking tour includes forty historic buildings, houses, and sites. There is a five-mile trail and a boardwalk observation deck that is perfect for walking, jogging, or bicycling. Fishing is permitted on the boardwalk. Charter fishing trips and boat rentals are available at the marina. Factory Creek Boat Ramp is a public boat ramp. Beaufort River, US 21, Port Royal Island.

Stay at **The Beaufort Lodge**. 1630 Ribaut Road, Port Royal. (843) 524-5600.

Dine at **The Back Porch Grill**, which has a varied menu and daily specials. Port Royal Landing Marina. (843) 525-9824.

The local favorite for dining is **11 Street Dockside**. (843) 524-7433.

Most area islands and attractions are less than fifteen minutes away, including Hunting Island State Park and Penn Center on St. Helena Island. Some islands, such as Distant, Deer, Dataw, and Polawana, are nothing more than exclusive residential developments.

Distant Island is the closest private residential island to downtown Beaufort, just 3 miles away. The island has a gazebo, tennis courts, nature trails, picnic areas, and bike trails that extend into town. (843) 524-0075 and info@distant-island.com.

Polawana is a private island offering just 40 5-acre homesites. (843) 524-7887, (877) 524-7788, and www.polawanaisland.com.

Deer Island has twenty-nine marsh and deep-water homesites, with prices starting in the upper $300,000s. (800) 417-6770, (877)-33-ISLANDS, and (843) 524-0010.

DATAW ISLAND

Six miles east of Beaufort lies Dataw Island, an exclusive, private, 870-acre community. It has been named one of the country's top retirement communities by *New Choices* magazine. Homesites start at $50,000 and homes at $200,000. The island is bounded to the east, west, and south by Jenkins Creek, and to the north by Morgan River. When finished, there will be 1,100 villas, patio homes, and large houses on the island. The gated community has twenty-four-hour security, two golf courses designed by Tom Fazio and Arthur Hills, eight Har-Tru tennis courts, a swimming pool, a marina, a 16,000-square-foot clubhouse with upscale restaurant and grill, a playground, a picnic pavilion, and walking trails. Accommodations are limited, but there are some one- and two-bedroom villas for rent. (800) 848-3838, (843) 838-3838, and www.discover-dataw.com.

COOSAW ISLAND

This small rural and residential island is on the Coosaw-Morgan River. There's nothing of interest to tourists, except that ACE Basin Tours provide ecology tours that depart from Coosaw Island Marina. (888) 814-3129, (843) 521-3099, and www.acebasintours.com. $.

KNOWLES ISLAND

This is another small island with little of interest to tourists except Palm Key. Palm Key is a large cottage that has rooms, suites, and cottages for rent and sale. It operates like a bed and breakfast, and guests staying in the cottages may opt to have family-style meals delivered to them or join other guests in the Palm Key dining room. All cottages have kitchens and are fully equipped with dishes and linens. Palm Key has won awards for its nature-based tourism and guests can choose from many activities: shrimping, crabbing, fly fishing, kayaking, canoeing, birding, wildflower photography, nature walks, and classes or lectures on low-country cooking or Gullah history. There is even a "beautifully designed and constructed labrinyth in a quiet forest of huge live oaks." Nightly rates or nature get-away packages are offered, and individuals, families, and groups are welcome. (800) 288-8420, (843) 726-6468, and www.palmkey.com.

T O U R I S M   I N F O R M A T I O N
Greater Beaufort Chamber of Commerce and Visitors Center. 1106 Carteret Street, Beaufort, SC 29901. (800) 638-3525, (843) 524-3163, and www.beaufortsc.org.

D I R E C T I O N S   &   A C C E S S I B I L I T Y
Take I-95 South, exit 33 to 17 North to 21 South into Beaufort, or take I-95 North, exit 8 to 170 North into Beaufort. If coming from Charleston, be sure to take the 526 Bypass. Beaufort is 45 miles from Savannah, Georgia; 70 miles from Charleston; and roughly a four-hour drive from Myrtle Beach.

If the bridge linking outer islands to Beaufort goes up, traffic often backs up on Bay Street and in the historic district. It went up four times in an hour and a half the last time I was in Beaufort! Most of the state's accessible islands are joined to the mainland by bridges or causeways. Some of the bridges have to be raised to accommodate Intracoastal Waterway traffic, so visitors need to accept this inconvenience as being another facet of island life.

✍ LADY'S ISLAND

Population: 9,321

Like most of the area's sea islands, this fifty-three-square mile island was used by planters until the Civil War. In 1891, an oyster factory was opened here by Captain Thomas Swinton, who later sold it to R. K. Harley. The oyster industry kept island inhabitants employed for many years. A bridge was constructed in 1927 that joined the wide island to the mainland. Soon thereafter, the Colony Gardens resort was built and rich Northerners began frequenting Lady's Island. The resort had a large two-story porch and a saltwater swimming pool behind the clubhouse. Since Colony Gardens opened in 1931, tourists have come from near and far to enjoy the charming island and all it has to offer, including numerous retail shops and businesses.

ACTIVITIES
Lady's Island Marina. (843) 522-0430 and www.ladysislandmarina.com.

Marsh Harbor Boat Yard. (843) 521-1500.

Sam's Point Boat Ramp is a public boat ramp on Lucy Point Creek, Lady's Island. US 21 to Route 802 East.

Brickyard Creek. Take US 21 to Route 802 East to Route 750 West to Route 72 East.

Lady's Island Boat Ramp is also a public boat ramp on Highway 21, just across Woods Memorial Bridge.

Broomfield Stables & Tack Shop offers horseback riding. (843) 521-1212.

Country Club of Beaufort is a par-72, Russell Breeden–designed, tournament-level golf course. Open to the public. Lady's Island, Pleasant Point Plantation. (843) 522-1605 and (800) 869-1617.

ENTERTAINMENT & NIGHTLIFE
The only entertainment is what is offered by island restaurants and the country club.

RESTAURANTS
Lady's Island Country Club is open to the public for lunch Tuesday-Saturday and dinner from 5:30 P.M.-8 P.M., Friday. The bar is open until 11 P.M. Reservations are requested. 139 Francis Marion Circle. (843) 522-9700.

Steamer Oyster & Steak House features local seafood prepared any way you want it and lowcountry seafood cuisine in a casual atmosphere.

A Lady's Island sunset Greater Beaufort Chamber of
Commerce

Open Monday-Saturday. 168 Sea Island Parkway. (843) 522-0210.

Fuji Restaurant is at 81 Sea Island Parkway. (843) 524-2662.

Ollie's Seafood Restaurant & Bar offers indoor and outdoor water-front dining. The menu includes local seafood (oysters are their specialty), pasta, and daily specials. Lunch and dinner are served daily. 71 Sea Island Parkway. (843) 525-6333.

Whitehall Plantation has a full-service restaurant. White Hall Drive. (843) 521-1700.

T O U R I S M I N F O R M A T I O N
Greater Beaufort Chamber of Commerce and Visitors Center. 1106 Carteret Street, Beaufort, SC 29901. (800) 638-3525 or (843) 524-3163, and www.beaufortsc.org.

D I R E C T I O N S & A C C E S S I B I L I T Y
Lady's Island is the closest island to Beaufort. It is just before St.

Helena's Island and Dataw Island, all joined to the mainland by the Parkway. Take Sea Island Parkway from Beaufort by heading south on Carteret Street, or take Highway 281 to Lady's Island Drive, which takes visitors across Port Royal Sound and on to the western side of Lady's Island.

☞ ☞ ☞

Gullah basket weaving originated in Africa and was brought to America by slaves. Baskets made of sweet grass were in big demand on the plantations for storage of breads, fruits, clothes, household items, crops, and for selling at market. Because younger Gullahs are not interested in learning to make baskets and Gullahs won't pass their knowledge to non-Gullahs, the weaving is a vanishing skill. Sweet grass baskets sold at roadside stands can cost as much as $150-$200. In addition to bringing along their skills at making intricate baskets, quilts, and shrimp nets, Gullahs brought over their fascinating but little-known beliefs and traditions. It is difficult to learn about Gullahs because their language is hard to understand, and they will only share so much information with outsiders. I did come across some insightful information in *Folk-Lore of the Sea Island, South Carolina.* Here are some Gullah sayings:

Dream
"Dream 'bout snakes, have somet'in' to fight, some kin' tem'tation."

Weather-signs
"Ef a cat wash her face, it goin' to rain."

Luck
"De firs' time you sleep in a strange house, make a wish, an' it comes true."

Health
For general ailments, a dime with a hole in it is tied around the ankle. For a headache, a string is tied around the head.

☜ ☜ ☜

✍ S t .   H e l e n a   I s l a n d

Population: 20,000

St. Helena has a grim, complex history. It was the first attempt at a New World settlement, the origin of slave trading, and an asylum for those seeking religious freedom. The first white man to lay claim to this island was Francisco Gordillo, an explorer who had been sent by seven wealthy Spaniards. He came ashore here on August 18, 1520, which was St. Helen's Day. In honor of that saint, Gordillo not only proclaimed the land for Spain, but called it Santa Elena (St. Helen). Gordillo and his expedition were warmly greeted by the Indians, who brought them ashore, showed them around, and shared food with the men. Gordillo reciprocated by inviting the natives out to his ships, but instead of providing them with a good meal and trinkets, he set sail with his first group of slaves. The Indians never made it to Hispaniola, where they were to work the gold mines, because the ships were lost at sea. Huguenots arrived at St. Helena, hoping to escape religious persecution. Instead, most were killed by Spanish Catholics. The original settlers either died of famine, died of fever, or fled. This island served as an outpost for the Spanish until 1587. Franciscan friars set up missions all along the coast, from Florida to Santa Elena. However, the priests were heavily restricted by the Spanish government. Spain was only interested in colonizing natives, particularly in regards to education and agriculture.

The next significant impact came in 1663 when English explorer William Hilton arrived and claimed the area for England. Once again, the Indians welcomed the white man and shared their land and resources. The first English settler to call St. Helena Island home was Thomas Nairn. He had a plantation on the south side of the island in 1698. More and more land grants were given as colonists arrived. By 1707, the Indians were ordered to confine themselves to a reservation that extended from the upper end of the Combahee River to the Savannah River. Most of the Indians on the islands were Yamasees who had been helpful to the English, so part of St. Helena (Polawana Island) was set aside as a small reservation for them.

The first white child was born on St. Helena in 1700. Because of the remoteness of the island, most planters also maintained residences in Beaufort or Charleston. Because there were no stores or doctors on the island, some plantation owners chose not to live on the island at all and left daily management to their overseers. The most direct route to St. Helena was across Lady's Island and the only way to get there was by boat. A rudimentary bridge linking these two islands was built in 1744.

Most islanders were Episcopalians who attended St. Helena

Many Beaufort residents earn a living catching shrimp. Greater Beaufort Chamber of Commerce

Episcopal Church in Beaufort. By 1740, there was a chapel on the island. By the 19th century, Beaufort area islands, including St. Helena, had made planters wealthy. In 1850, St. Helena cultivated more than one million pounds of cotton. Population swelled. Several service organizations, such as the St. Helena Agricultural Society and St. Helena Mounted Riflemen, were formed. When the Civil War took place, planters and their families left St. Helena and other area islands for safer places. The slaves who remained either went into hiding or continued their duties until food rations ran out. Rumors abounded across the state that the Union Army occupied certain South Carolina sea islands and anyone seeking refuge would be protected. Many people, especially women and children, died of exposure, starvation, or drowning, before they made it to the islands. Those who survived the journey were sent to Edisto Island or St. Helena Island. Whatever the military didn't use or consume, the refugees were allowed to have.

After the war, many plantations were sold to Northerners, who used the land for hunting. Marsh tackies, a nickname given to the tough, little horses with extremely curly hair, freely roamed St. Helena. When it was populated, the horses were used to pull wagons over dirt roads on the island. Teachers, preachers, and missionaries arrived at St. Helena and founded Penn School in 1862 for freed island slaves. Youths were taught important skills, including reading, writing, farming, construction, and cooking. A public school opened on the island in the late 1940s and in 1953, Penn School became Penn Center. The former school became a center for reform, tackling all kinds of issues that impacted blacks. Dr. Martin Luther King Jr. came to Penn Center in 1963 to meet with other black leaders and plan his march on Washington.

St. Helena is one of the largest sea islands in the state. Today, the fifteen-mile long and eight-mile wide island is mainly agricultural. It grows more tomatoes than any other place in South Carolina.

TOURS & ATTRACTIONS

Fripp Plantation, also known as Seaside Plantation, circa 1800. John Fripp was given St. Helena Island by King William III in return for his efforts in England's war against Spain. Edgar Fripp inherited the island and Seaside Plantation just before the Civil War. The Fripps had to leave St. Helena because of the war and the house was taken over by Federal troops, along with many other area plantation homes. The Union used these houses in their Port Royal Experiment, which was a federal government program to educate former slaves (freedmen). The General Superintendent of the Port Royal Experiment lived at Seaside. Later, Edgar Fripp was able to resume possession of his home and 732 of the 1,284 acres he had owned. The land was sold and used as a hunting sanctuary in 1920 and then as a farm. Fripp Plantation is not open to the public.

St. Helena's Episcopal Church of Beaufort was established in 1712 and eventually used as a Union hospital. Troops dug up gravestones to use as operating tables. Free.

Tombee Plantation, circa 1790. This structure has served as a home, beauty parlor, and nightclub. It has been moved from its original location on the river to Station Creek and restored. Tombee Plantation is not open to the public.

White Church "Chapel of Ease" ruins, circa 1740, was built for St. Helena planters. It was destroyed by fire in 1865, but some of the structure survived, as well as some large tombs and a cemetery.

Penn Center & York W. Bailey Museum details the history of Penn Center and of the Gullah culture. Originally used as a school, it was established in 1862 for freed island slaves by Laura Towne, an abolitionist and Unitarian. It later served as a center of reform. Cultural programs and lectures are given here, and dorm rooms and cottages are available. Open Monday-Friday, except holidays. Martin Luther King Drive. (843) 838-8560. $.

Handmade Gullah sweetgrass baskets. Greater
Beaufort Chamber of Commerce

Gullah-N-Geechie Tour is a two-hour bus tour of St. Helena Island, including the Penn Center. (843) 838-7516 and (843) 838-6312. $.
"Rev's" Step on Gullah Tours. St. Helena Island. (843) 838-3185. $.

NATURE & WILDLIFE
The Kayak Farm takes visitors on half-day and all-day wilderness explorations of the ACE Basin and Hunting Island State Park, departing from St. Helena Island. Open daily, except holidays. 1289 Sea Island Parkway. (843) 838-2008 and thekayakfarm@islc.net. $

Cap'n Wally offers fishing and diving excursions, as well as nature cruises. Sign up at the Shrimp Shack. (843) 525-1174. $

ENTERTAINMENT & NIGHTLIFE
Minimal, but Beaufort is less than ten minutes away.

ACCOMMODATIONS
Royal Frogmore Inn. Highway 21 East, 863 Sea Island Parkway. (843) 838-5400.

BEAUFORT ISLANDS

VACATION RENTALS
Harbor Island Rentals. 2123 Sea Island Parkway, #B, St. Helena, SC 29920. (800) 553-0251 and (843) 838-4800.

Harbor Island Sales & Accommodations. 2 Harbor Drive, St. Helena, SC 29920. (800) 809-2410 and (843) 838-2410.

CAMPGROUNDS
Tuck in the Wood Campground is on Lands End Road, just 12 miles from Hunting Island State Park and public beach. Full hook-ups are available. (843) 838-CAMP and (843) 838-2267.

RESTAURANTS
Shrimp Shack. 1929 Sea Island Parkway. (843) 838-2962.

Ultimate Eating Restaurant. 859 Sea Island Parkway. (843) 838-2402.

Johnson Creek Restaurant & Tavern. 2141 Sea Island Parkway. (843) 838-4166.

PJ's Pizza & Subs is at the island Welcome Center, just before the Shrimp Shack. (843) 838-5555.

Russell's Roadhouse has New England style seafood, including whole lobsters. 1760 Sea Island Parkway. (843) 838-0821.

Gay Fish Company, across the street from Shrimp Shack on Sea Island Parkway, sells fresh seafood.

FESTIVALS & ANNUAL EVENTS
Penn Center Heritage Days Celebration (November). (843) 838-8580.

Candlelight Walking Tour (March). E. C. W. Tours. (843) 524-0363.

Low country Driving Tour (March). E. C. W. Tours. (843) 524-0363.

TOURISM INFORMATION
Greater Beaufort Chamber of Commerce and Visitors Center. 1106 Carteret Street, Beaufort, SC 29901. (800) 638-3525, (843) 524-3163, and www.beaufortsc.org.

DIRECTIONS & ACCESSIBILITY
I-95 to exit 33 to US 21 into Beaufort. In Beaufort, follow US 21 Business for 10 miles to St. Helena Island.

❧ C AT I SLAND

Population: approximately 225 homes

Cat Island is a 423-acre barrier island that was briefly home to a nudist colony but is now primarily residential. It offers no tours, attractions, or nightlife—just beautiful scenery and lots of peace and quiet.

There is a new seventy-five-homesite development, Old Tabby Park (on South Carolina National golf course). Homesites start at $39,900 and houses cost $200,000 or more. (843) 322-1000.

A CTIVITIES

There are a couple of golf courses: **Secession Golf Club,** which is private and **South Carolina National,** a championship golf course designed by George Cobb. While the public is permitted golfing privileges, they are not allowed to use other club amentites. (800) 221-9582 and (843) 524-0300.

A CCOMMODATIONS

Beaulieu House is a picturesque bed and breakfast overlooking the waterway that has a family suite and six guest rooms, each with private

Beaulieu House is a bed-and-breakfast inn on Cat Island. Terrance Zepke

baths and porches. The exterior is bright pink with white trim and green shutters. It looks like an oversized dollhouse. And, speaking of toys, the owner has an extensive toy collection displayed for guests to enjoy. Lowcountry breakfast is included and deep-water dockage is available for boaters. 3 Sheffield Court, at the end of Island Causeway, Cat Island. (843) 770-0303, (843) 575-0303, and beaulieubb@aol.com.

TOURISM INFORMATION
Greater Beaufort Chamber of Commerce and Visitors Center. 106 Carteret Street, Beaufort, SC 29901. (800) 638-3525, (843) 524-3163, and www.beaufortsc.org.

DIRECTIONS & ACCESSIBILITY
This island is 5 miles from Beaufort. Most of Cat Island is open to the public and visitors should restrict themselves to tourist destinations, including Beaulieu House and South Carolina National.

☞ BEAR ISLAND

Population: uninhabited

Bear Island is a designated Wildlife Management Area in Colleton County. Situated between the Ashepoo and Edisto Rivers, it contains 12,021 acres of marshland and lots of wildlife, especially shorebirds and wading birds. Ducks are abundant in the winter and songbirds in the spring and fall. Avocets, black-necked stilts, eagles, alligators, and many varieties of reptiles and amphibians are often spotted. Many hard-to-find plants, including carnivorous pitcher-plants and orchids, can be found here. Hunting is permitted in accordance with state regulations, but a permit is required by law. Fishing, crabbing, and camping are allowed seasonally, but never swimming. Insect repellent is highly recommended. Be observant and respectful of alligators and snakes. There are some venomous snakes in this wildlife area. Walking and biking (preferably off-

Bear Island is a great place to fish. Terrance Zepke

road or with mountain bikes) is the best way to get around. Tours can be arranged by contacting Bear Island Wildlife Management.

Tourism Information
Bear Island Wildlife Management Area. 585 Donnelley Drive, Green Pond. (843) 844-8957 and (843) 844-2952.

Directions & Accessibility
Bear Island is open Monday-Saturday, January 21-October 31, during daylight hours. It is 13 miles off Highway 17 on Bennett's Point Road. Three miles northeast of Green Pond. Follow the signs from Highway 17. Free.

𝒽 Harbor Island

Population: 50

Harbor Island is probably one of the most alluring beach communities in the state because of its convenient location near Beaufort and

This is a typical Harbor Island house. Terrance Zepke

Hilton Head. It has a pretty beach and homesites that start in the low $40,000s—a bargain in a state where island homesites (with or without beaches) usually start at $250,000-$500,000! This small, private barrier island on the Atlantic Ocean has no organized tours or attractions. What this place offers is tranquillity and panoramic vistas, including a beach with lots of sea oats and dunes, although dunes are minimal on the north end. Wading birds and shorebirds, including heron and egret rookeries, can also be found on the island.

ACTIVITIES
Harbor Island has roughly 3 miles of beach, which is more than enough for swimming, sunning, crabbing, fishing, shelling, and beach-combing.

Guests staying on the island are permitted access to the **Harbor Island Resort Beach & Racquet Club**. The club offers tennis, swimming, a playground, and fitness center, as well as a pro shop, deli, bar, and café that is open seasonally. Resort guests are permitted to play the two golf courses on nearby Fripp Island: Ocean Point and Ocean Creek. Kids staying at Harbor Island Resort may also participate in Camp Fripp and all organized programs and amenities offered at Fripp Island Resort. (843) 838-7345. $

ENTERTAINMENT & NIGHTLIFE
Entertainment is mostly restricted to what Fripp or Harbor Island

resers offer.

Johnson Creek Restaurant & Tavern offers weekend entertainment. 2141 Sea Island Parkway. (843) 838-4166. $

A C C O M M O D A T I O N S
Harbor Island Accommodations has sixty villas available for daily, weekly, and monthly rental. Two Harbor Drive. (800) 809-2410 and (843) 838-2410.

Harbor Island Rentals offers seventy homes and villas available for daily, weekly, and monthly rental. The best rates are the seasonal specials, including winter and summer Early Bird or Indian Summer deals. 2123-B Sea Island Parkway. (800) 553-0251, (843) 838-4800, and www.harborisland-sc.com.

R E S T A U R A N T S
Dining facilities include eateries at **Harbor Island Resort** and **Fripp Island Resort**.

Johnson Creek Restaurant & Tavern offers casual dining, local seafood, and weekend entertainment. Open for dinner only, Monday-Saturday. On the causeway leading to the island, 2141 Sea Island Parkway. (843) 838-4166.

Harbor Island General Store has food and drinks, picnic and beach supplies, camping and grilling items, and an ABC package store. 2087 Sea Island Parkway, located just beyond entrance check-in. (843) 838-9799.

T O U R I S M I N F O R M A T I O N
Greater Beaufort Chamber of Commerce and Visitors Center. 1106 Carteret Street, Beaufort, SC 29901. (800) 638-3525, (843) 524-3163, and www.beaufortsc.org.

D I R E C T I O N S & A C C E S S I B I L I T Y
Harbor Island is a private, gated island located 14 miles east of Beaufort on Sea Island Parkway/Highway 21.

✐ H U N T I N G   I S L A N D

Population: uninhabited

The island is one mile wide and three miles long. It earned its name because it was once used as a hunting retreat by area planters. The island remained privately owned until the 1920s when all the owners, except for two, sold their land to the government. By 1933, the last two private landowners sold their property. Five years later, Hunting Island State Park was established. The island, which is situated on St. Helena Sound, has abundant wildlife, waterfowl, deer, sea oats, salt marsh, cabbage palmettos, pine-palmetto trees, and 125 species of birds

The causeway connecting the island to the mainland was built by the Civilian Conservation Corps (CCC) in the late 1930s and early 1940s. The men who worked on the project were called mud puppies because they had to manually dig out thousands of buckets of mud to build the road. There were no backhoes or heavy machinery.

Until the 1970s, visitors could drive on the beach. In fact, cars used to pull right up alongside a picnic table and claim the area for the day. Campers often brought several coolers to hold all the fish and crabs they caught. At that time, the beaches were much wider, but erosion has taken its toll.

Erosion is a problem in all coastal areas, but it has hit Hunting Island especially hard. As I discussed in *Lighthouses of the Carolinas*, barrier

Plaque found at entrance to the beach that explains the severity of Hunting Island's erosion problem. Terrance Zepke

Hunting Island beach Greater Beaufort Chamber
of Commerce

islands are ever-changing, shifting ribbons of sand. They are always reshaping themselves, for better or for worse. Hunting Island averages 15 feet of beach erosion every year, which is the highest of all the South Carolina islands. Between 1830 and 1875, over half a mile of its northern tip eroded. Another seven-tenths of a mile was gone by 1930. The average annual rate of erosion has been calculated to be 25 feet on the northern tip and 10 feet on the central beach. Factors affecting erosion rates include size and proximity of shoals, how the waves hit the beach, and water currents. On Hunting Island, waves break to the north and south, which means instead of redepositing sand back onto the beach, the currents carry it away. The National Park Service is doing what it can to address the erosion problem by forbidding visitors from walking on dunes and by building drift fences, which keep sand from being carried off by wind and water.

Hunting Island State Park is 5,000 acres with 4 miles of beach, a lagoon, and 8 miles of nature trails through a wildlife refuge that permits camping. The park has two hundred campsites and fifteen two- or three-bedroom cabins for rent. No pets are allowed in the cabins, but they are allowed on the island as long as they are on leashes that are 6 feet or less. Park cabins are heavily sought after, which is not hard to imagine if you

Hunting Island Lighthouse is the crown jewel of Huntung Island State Park. Terrance Zepke

realize that roughly one million visitors come to this state park annually. The large influx of visitors receive their information by word-of-mouth or are repeat visitors. A lottery, using all applications submitted to date, is held at the beginning of March. Stays are restricted to one week at a time. There is usually a line waiting when gates open in the summertime.

TOURS & ATTRACTIONS

Hunting Island State Park is open daily. 2555 Sea Island Parkway. (843) 838-2011. $

Hunting Island Lighthouse was built in 1875. The first beacon was erected in 1859 but was destroyed during the Civil War. Hunting Island Lighthouse is part of the state park and is the only South Carolina lighthouse open to visitors. $

ACTIVITIES

Fishing, shelling, swimming, sunbathing, strolling, relaxing, wildlife viewing, and much more can be accomplished at Hunting Island, but hunting is not permitted. There is a Visitors Center, near the entrance, that houses island exhibits. The Nature Center at the fishing pier also has displays pertaining to the island's history and ecology. Additionally, there are some seasonally organized activities led by a naturalist. Fishing (bass, trout, whiting, and drum) is permitted at the lagoon and the pier. There are some walking trails and a boardwalk that leads out to the salt marsh. Restrooms, picnic shelters, a boat ramp, parking, and pay phones can all be found on the island.

NATURE & WILDLIFE

Alligators, bottle-nosed dolphins, otters, minks, raccoons, deer, loggerhead sea turtles, and many species of birds can be spotted. There are several eco-systems, including maritime forest, marsh, and beach.

RESTAURANTS

There are no restaurants on the island, but there is a convenience store at the campground entrance that carries ice, groceries, film, and souvenirs. There is another store near the lighthouse that offers the same items on a seasonal basis.

TOURISM INFORMATION

Hunting Island State Park. 2555 Sea Island Parkway. (843) 838-2011 and (843) 838-7437.

Greater Beaufort Chamber of Commerce and Visitors Center. 1106 Carteret Street, Beaufort, SC 29901. (800) 638-3525, (843) 524-3163, and www.beaufortsc.org.

DIRECTIONS & ACCESSIBILITY

The island is connected to the mainland by an elevated highway across the marsh and Intracoastal Waterway. Sixteen miles east of Beaufort on Highway 21. Roughly halfway between Charleston and Savannah, GA.

BEAUFORT ISLANDS

ꙮ FRIPP ISLAND

Population: 700-900

Nineteen miles southeast of Beaufort, on Fripp's Inlet, lies Fripp Island. The 3,000-acre island was used for hunting by the Yamasee Indians and later acquired by English Captain Johannes Fripp, who was a hero in battles against the French and Spanish and also a privateer. King George granted him the island as payment for services rendered to the Crown.

During the Civil War, Fripp Island was appropriated by the Federals for back taxes. The $6.67 debt was subsequently paid by Julia Prioleau and the land was returned. The first major development occurred in the 1960s. Jack L. Kilgore, who owned the island, arranged for a bridge to be built, linking Fripp to Hunting Island. The $500,000 bridge was finished in 1964. Paths were cleared and wild animals (mainly boars) were contained. The island was then more appealing for residential development. Luxury homes and villas were built, and a harmonious balance with the island's ecology has been maintained. Author Pat Conroy has a home here and the beautiful island has been used as a backdrop in several movies, including *The Jungle Book* and *Forrest Gump*.

Primary island transportation is walking, bicycling, and golf carts. Bikes and carts can be rented by the day or the week.

TOURS & ATTRACTIONS
Captain Eddie's Fishing Charters & Sightseeing Cruises. (843-838-

Wildlife, especially deer, are often spotted in the front lawn or backyard of residences. Terrance Zepke

View of some Fripp Island home docks and watercraft. Islanders utilize the waterway the way most of us use roads and highways. Terrance Zepke

3782) Tours, including dolphin watching, depart from Fripp Island Marina (843-838-1517). $

ACTIVITIES

There are lots of walking and nature trails where you will find deer, stately palmetto trees, and huge sea oats. In addition to the residential communities, there is **Fripp Island Resort** and more than 3 miles of beach. The resort has a Beach Club, which contains swimming pools, a fitness center, tennis courts, bicycle paths (bike rentals are available), fishing off Paradise Pier, and three championship golf courses (one of which is on adjacent Cat Island). Boats can be rented at the marina and nature/dolphin-watching and fishing excursions are offered. There are a few shops and one gallery. Organized resort activities include Camp Fripp children's program, various family adventures, a kids' night out, and teen activities. (843) 838-1516 and (843) 838-1517.

The resort has been named one of the "100 Best Golf Resorts in North America" by *Links*. All courses require soft spikes or spikeless shoes, which are available for rent in the pro shop. Ocean Creek Golf Course has won "Top 10 New Course Design" from *Golf* and *The Golfer*. Lodging, golf and tennis packages, and reduced rates from November through February are available.

NATURE & WILDLIFE

The island is home to many species of birds, alligators, deer, and raccoons.

Camp Fripp is the activities center for Fripp Island Resort, which has programs for kids and teens. Terrance Zepke

ENTERTAINMENT & NIGHTLIFE
Entertainment is limited to what is offered by island restaurants and Fripp Island Resort.

ACCOMMODATIONS
DuBose Rentals has about a dozen homes and villas available for rent. 804 Washington Street, Beaufort. (877) 768-7999 and (843) 838-3535.

Fripp Island Resort has over three hundred villas and homes available for rental. 1 Tarpon Blvd. (800) 845-4100, (843) 845-4102, (843) 838-3535, (843) 838-3712, and www.frippislandresort.com.

Resort Properties has many villas for rent. 2143 Sea Island Parkway. (800) 858-7595 and (843) 838-7595.

RESTAURANTS
There are several places to eat at Fripp Island Resort, including The Ocean Grill, Bonito Boathouse at the marina, Peg Leg's Food & Spirits, 19th Hole, Hugo's Café & Deli, Lil' Dipper Café, and Sandbar.

FESTIVALS & ANNUAL EVENTS
Spring Festival (April).
Bass Fishing Tournament (October).
Laser Sailing Regatta (May).

N E A R B Y   P O I N T S   O F   I N T E R E S T
Hunting Island State Park (see page 149.)
Port Royal Island (see page 130.)
St. Helena Island (see page 135–140.)

T O U R I S M   I N F O R M A T I O N
The Fripp Company/Resort. One Tarpon Boulevard, Fripp Island. (800) 845-4100 and www.frippislandresort.com.
Greater Beaufort Chamber of Commerce and Visitors Center. 1106 Carteret Street, Beaufort, SC 29901. (800) 638-3525, (843) 524-3163, and www.beaufortsc.org.

D I R E C T I O N S   &   A C C E S S I B I L I T Y
Fripp is 19 miles east of Beaufort. Stop at the front desk of the resort and request a pass if you are considering renting and would like a preliminary look. Visitors may eat at Hugo's Tavern on the Tee, but only resort guests and property owners may dine at other island eateries. Hugo's is a café and deli with a casual atmosphere.

Going South: Take I-95 to exit 33 to US 21. Follow the signs for Beaufort and cross the bridge onto Fripp Island.

Going North: Take exit 8 and turn right. Follow the signs for Beaufort. Turn left onto John Smith Road. Take a left on Highway 170 and 278. Stay on Highway 170 when the road splits. Take a right onto Highway 802, and go past Parris Island. Turn right at the first light. Follow Highway 802 over Lady's Island Bridge. Turn right at Highway 21 and cross Fripp Island Bridge.

✍ P A R R I S   I S L A N D

In the 16th century, French and Spanish settlements were founded on much of this island, which is situated in the Broad River. The first colonists, French Huguenots, were brought here by Captain Jean Ribaut in 1562. The settlement, Charlesfort, struggled to survive in this new place. When

More than 20,000 recruits train every year at the U.S. Marine Corps Recruit Depot on Parris Island. Terrance Zepke

Captain Ribaut was sent to France for food, the settlers grew desperate during his absence. Illness and Indians threatened their existence to the point that they built a boat and set sail. They perished at sea. For many years, the French, Spanish, and English fought over who would own the island. The English finally won control of Parris Island.

It was named after Alexander Parris, who was a state treasurer. The four-and-a-half-mile long and six-mile wide island became a naval installation in 1876 and a prison in 1906. The prison closed in the 1930s. A training facility for the United States Marine Corps was established here in 1915 when the government bought the entire island for $248,328. It is the largest training and recruiting base on the East Coast. Approximately 20,000 recruits are trained every year at the US Marine Corps Recruit Depot at Parris Island. Because this island is a military installation, there are no civilian activities or accommodations. **Note: Since September 11, 2001, Parris Island has been closed indefinitely to all visitors. Before that, tours and attractions accomodated over 100, 000 visitors yearly. Visiting information is listed here in case the base opens to tourists once again. Call to verify.**

TOURS & ATTRACTIONS

Douglas Visitor Center is open daily. (843) 228-3650 and (843) 228-3297. Free.

USMC Museum is a 10,000-square-foot military museum, theater,

Parris Island U.S.M.C. Museum. Terrance Zepke

and archives open to the public. Guided tours of the base are offered. Open daily, except holidays. (843) 228-3650 and www.parrisisland.com. Free.

Santa Elena/Charlesfort records the history of the French and Spanish settlements on Parris Island. The historic site contains exhibits and archaeological monuments of these early European colonies. There is also a nature trail, and archaeological work is sometimes conducted at the site located near Parris Island Military Museum.

Self-Guided Driving Tour of Parris Island. (843) 228-3650.

Parris Island Bus Tours provides tours of the base. (843) 228-3650 and (843) 228-3297.

T O U R I S M   I N F O R M A T I O N
Greater Beaufort Chamber of Commerce and Visitors Center. 1106 Carteret Street, Beaufort, SC 29901. (800) 638-3525, (843) 524-3163, and www.beaufortsc.org.

D I R E C T I O N S   &   A C C E S S I B I L I T Y
Take Highway 281 until it ends. The bridge connects the mainland to Parris Island. Once you drive onto the island, military rules and regulations supersede civilian rights. For example, car searches are sometimes conducted as training exercises.

ᕵ SPRING ISLAND

Population: 400-500 families

This 3,000-acre sea island was once used by Indians for hunting and fishing. A land grant was issued in 1706 to Scotsman John Cochran, who set up an Indian trading post on the island. Cochran's Indian trading and other ruthless dealings contributed to the Yemasee War, a bloody massacre of nearly one hundred settlers by the Indians. The island remained in the Cochran family for the next two hundred years. One of the heirs was George Edwards who lived from the late 1700s to 1859. The ruins of his home still exist on Spring Island.

Probably one-half to three-fourths of Spring Island was producing the premium-grade Sea Island cotton until the Civil War and the boll weevil struck the state. The Civil War devastated much of South Carolina, and Spring Island was no exception. The fields and mansions lay in ruins after the war. Things improved when wealthy Northerners began using it as a hunting retreat. As was often the case after the war, land was sold to well-to-do Northerners by Southerners who had lost their fortunes during the war. It was owned from 1902 to 1912 by the Spring Island Barony Club. Alice M. Townsend owned it from 1912 to 1920, when it was sold to

This is the outdoor communal area where picnics and parties are held.
Terrance Zepke

❦ ❦ ❦

"The developers of Spring Island, a high-end golf/residential
community on the coast of South Carolina, make nature the
most important amenity."
—*Urban Land,* June 1996

"On Spring Island, preservation is more than just a lofty,
abstract idea . . . it is an ongoing, active ritual of devotion,
carefully conceived and meticulously executed."
—*Beaufort Low Country,* Winter 1995

"Nature rules on this Carolina sea island, where residents enjoy nature
walks, sea kayaking, and fishing. Estate lots are required to be set back
100 feet from the water and 50 feet from the road. A sanctioned
arborist cuts limbs to provide a view from the house while minimizing
its visibility to passersby . . . With the sensibilities of small town residents, island dwellers share swimming and tennis facilities, as well as
a stable of horses for rent. A community garden supplies fresh produce
for the island's dining room."
—*Coastal Living,* May 1997

❦ ❦ ❦

Colonel William M. Copp, who had been a member of the barony club.

Copp built a large home on the southern end of the island in 1927
and set up a truck farming business on Spring Island. It was a prosperous
enterprise and soon fifty percent of the island was used for growing corn,
sweet potatoes, beans, lettuce, tomatoes, turnips, cabbage, pecans, and
cotton. Slave descendants worked the farms as tenant farmers, earning
$2.50 a week. These twenty to forty families lived for free in houses erect-
ed in the early 1900s by Copp. Each dwelling was painted red with white
trim. The Copp family later switched from produce to raising cattle and
hogs. At one time, the Copp homestead included the two-story house they
resided in, two tenant houses, a barn, a shed, a windmill, a generator and
battery house, a pump house, dog kennels, an ice plant, and a large dock.
Elsewhere on the island were the remaining tenant houses, a sawmill, a
planing mill, a grist mill, and a rice mill. Rice was planted to attract birds
for hunting. Commercial farming ended with William Copp's death in
1939. His widow, Otillie M. Copps Mills, sold the island in 1943.

According to Spring Island promotional material, "Twelve generations of private owners, spanning more than three centuries, have helped
to preserve, mold and enhance the land with a gentle passion which is
everywhere evident today."

❦ ❦ ❦

The Spring Island Philosophy—
"Spring Island will appeal most to those who come not to be seen,
but to *behold*; not to be heard by others, but to *listen*—to that special
wisdom which only natural and history can impart. Everywhere, the
emphasis will be on quiet enjoyment and casual, understated charm;
an escape from the pretension and formality which have come to
characterize too much of our daily lives. The future of Spring Island
must be approached not only as an opportunity, but as an *obligation*.
The cherished sense of a special place with which a dozen generations of owners have looked upon this land must never be allowed
to die."
—Spring Island [Developers] Sales Booklet

❦ ❦ ❦

More recently, Spring Island has been written up in many leading
publications for its successful blend of development and nature. In 1990,
the Spring Island trust, a nonprofit organization, was created by the Spring
Island Company, which bought the island that same year, in order to protect and preserve it. Over one-third of the island, 1,300 acres, is in trust
and referred to as the Nature Preserve. The trust is funded by a sales transfer fee; 1.5% of all homesite sales and 1% of all home sales are forever
contributed to the trust. According to the Spring Island Company, the trust
has three major functions: "to manage the Nature Preserve and other open
spaces, 2) to provide educational programs for members and guests, and
3) to consult with the developers—and eventually the Property Owner
Association—to implement sound developmental plans and land management and landscaping practices."

In keeping with the philosophy, the original plan for 5,500 homesites
was cut substantially to only four or five hundred. Additional requirements include deep setbacks for waterside homes, larger buffers between
houses and streets, large lots, and few paved roads. The same developers
were involved with planning adjoining Callawassie Island; Hilton Head's
Sea Pines Plantation; Snowmass Village, Colorado; Semiahmoo,
Washington; and Amelia Island, Florida.

TOURS & ATTRACTIONS

There are no organized tours or attractions, except the tabby ruins of
antebellum Edwards House, once owned by George Edwards, one of the
heirs of the original owner of island, John Cochran; and a statue of St.
Francis of Assisi.

Kayaking adventures and nature cruises begin at Wardels' Landing.
Terrance Zepke

ACTIVITIES

There is no beach on Spring Island. To compensate for this, property owners are offered croquet, baseball, horse shoes, a tree house, a gazebo, a picnic area with a large outdoor grill, a swimming pool, fishing, tennis, a championship golf course (Old Tabby Links was designed by Arnold Palmer and Ed Seay, and its signature 17th hole is set on a gorgeous peninsula bordered by marsh and palmettos), walking and hiking trails, canoeing, boating, and horse stables. There is also an off-island hunt club. Three full-time naturalists organize programs, such as sunset nature cruises, kayaking, crabbing, shrimping, and other field trips. Property owners may stay in one of the island's guest cottages until they decide to build.

At the reception center, Walking Landing, there is also the River House Restaurant, guest cottages, a sports garden, a summer house, a recreation center, horse stables, and a boat ramp. The Nature Center houses island artifacts, displays, and books on nature and bird-watching. Meals are served in the dining room and usually originate from the island, including shrimp, crab, venison, quail, and organically grown vegetables.

During my visit, I was given *Ten Great Places of Spring Island*. This spiral-bound publication highlights all the things that make the island a true paradise, including a mini-waterfall, Great Salt Pond, Shrimp Pond, and Muckel Bottom Marsh.

Walker House Reception Center. Terrance Zepke

NATURE & WILDLIFE
There are many species of flora and fauna. Wildlife includes bobcats, foxes, deer, armadillos, alligators, fox squirrels, otters, owls, frogs, insects, and many species of birds, including bald eagles and great blue herons.

SALES INFORMATION
Spring Island Sales. 42 Mobley Oaks Lane Spring Island, SC 29910. (843) 987-2073.

DIRECTIONS & ACCESSIBILITY
This is a private, gated island with twenty-four-hour security—only residents are permitted on the island. It is 15 miles south of Beaufort, 18 miles south of Hilton Head, and 30 miles from Savannah. To reach the island, residents cross Callawassie Island, which is also a private, residential community. It is not as exclusive as Spring Island, but it is rather idyllic with lots of marsh and lagoons. Property owners may join Callawassie Island Club, which has a Tom Fazio–designed golf course, the River Club with riverfront swimming pool, tennis courts, community boat dock, clubhouse with casual and fine dining, and many other amenities. Access to the 880-acre Callawassie Island is restricted to residents and there is a guard gate. For Callawassie sales queries call (800) 221-8431 and (843) 987-2100.

✑ HILTON HEAD ISLAND

Population: 33,000

It's interesting that this island's population has never exceeded what it was around the time of the Civil War when indigo, cotton, and rice plantations were prominent. This twelve-mile long and five-mile wide island formed as a result of thousands of years of heavily fluctuating sea levels and sand deposits carried by rivers from the Appalachian Mountains. It is the largest sea island between Florida and New Jersey. To the south is Calibogue Sound and Daufuskie Island, to the east is the Atlantic Ocean, and to the north is Port Royal Sound and the mainland.

The first residents were native Indians who lived here as early as 4000 B.C. Little is known about these people but evidence of their existence remains as part of the Sea Pines Forest Preserve. In the 1560s, French Huguenots, who left Europe to avoid persecution, lived briefly on the island before moving on to Beaufort. A group of West Indies landowners sent English seaman Captain William Hilton to explore Hilton Head Island in 1664. Partly to recognize the headlands that line Port Royal Sound and partly to honor Captain Hilton, the island was subsequently named Hilton Head. Before Captain Hilton's discovery, the island had other names, such as Punta de Santa Elena, Isla de los Osos (Island of the

This is a view of Hilton Head's Harbour Town Marina, which often accomodates enormous yachts and houseboats belonging to wealthy residents and tourists alike. Hilton Head, South Carolina Chamber of Commerce

Bears), and Ile de la Riviere Grande (Island of the Big River).

It was the end of the 17th century before English colonists settled permanently in the area. By the 1800s, vast indigo, rice, sugar cane, and cotton plantations had been established and had made a handful of families very wealthy. Sea Island cotton was extremely profitable. This kind of cotton was worth $54 a pound as opposed to regular cotton that only fetched $12 a pound. Unfortunately, British troops arrived in 1813 and destroyed most of these plantations. In 1861, these homes and fields were again ruined when 12,000 Union troops invaded Hilton Head during the Civil War's Battle of Port Royal, the biggest naval engagement of the war. As a result of this military engagement, the first American freedmen's village, Mitchelville, was established.

Those who remained after the War Between the States made a decent living fishing, oystering, and farming. In 1953, Hilton Head's first motel, the Sea Crest Motel, opened. It consisted of only two rooms until 1960 when it expanded to eight rooms. A bridge linking the island to the mainland was built in 1956 and electricity came to the island the following year. In 1960, beach-front lots went for $300. By 1978, that figure jumped to $150,000. Nowadays, that same property is easily worth five times that amount.

Today, roughly 2.5 million tourists flock to the island every year. What makes Hilton Head so appealing is its 19 miles of shoreline (including 12 miles of beaches) extending from Dolphin Head to South Beach, and the numerous outdoor activities available, such as biking, sailing, canoeing, kayaking, fishing, roller blading, horseback riding, and nature watching, as well as first rate golf courses and tennis courts. Additionally, there are many fine outlet stores, gift shops, department stores, and boutiques on the island.

Despite development, the island has managed to maintain the look and feel of a quaint coastal community by prohibiting neon signs and establishing strict building policies. All construction must be environmentally planned. The island has also managed to hold on to its cultural heritage. Descendants of slaves, known as Gullahs, praise their ancestral history through the Hallelujah Singers and annual events.

The best way to familiarize yourself with the island is to take a day tour; the island's toll road and traffic circles can be confusing to visitors. Also, most communities on the island are private and gated. The oldest communities are Sea Pines Plantation, Palmetto Dunes, Port Royal Plantation, Shipyard Plantation, and Hilton Head Plantation. These are also considered resorts and most contain marinas with shops and cafés, pools, tennis courts, and golf courses. Some places, such as the 5,000-acre Sea Pines Plantation, will let visitors purchase an inexpensive day pass so that they may enjoy these amenities.

Hilton Head is a beautful place any time of day, especially at sunrise and sunset. Hilton Head Chamber of Commerce

T O U R S   &   A T T R A C T I O N S

Discover Tours offers interesting tours of the island. (843) 726-9217. $.

Gray Line/Low Country Adventures, Ltd. provides both exciting island tours and other day trips to Savannah, Beaufort, and Charleston. Tours include evening haunted trolley tour and the explorer. (800) 845-5582, (843) 681-8212, and www.lowcountryadventures.com. For Savannah tours, call Gray Line at (912) 234-TOUR and (912) 234-8687. $.

Gullah Heritage Trail Tours gives short, insightful tours of places pertaining to the area's African-American culture. An ordinance was passed in 1991 that forbids eradication or vandalism of any Gullah structures, such as churches and segregated school houses. (843) 681-7066. $.

GULLAH-N-GEECHIE MAHN Tours explore Gullah history and heritage. (843) 838-7516). $.

Spirit of Harbour Town at Harbour Town offers narrated sunset dinner cruises. Reservations are required. (843) 842-7179. $.

Baynard Ruins at Sea Pines Plantation is the remains of a circa 1800 Lowcountry cotton plantation. William Baynard won 1,000 acres in a poker game and built a house on the land in 1830. Union forces burned the dwelling down in 1861 but remains of the house, Baynard Ruins, are on Sea Pines Plantation, near the intersection of Baynard Park Road and Plantation Drive. A self-guided tour provides an interesting glimpse into a bygone era. $.

Baynard Mausoleum, circa 1846, is an interesting site with a ghost

❧ ❧ ❧

Gullahs are descendants of West African slaves who worked on area plantations. After slavery ended, they remained on the island and became fishermen, hunters, and farmers. Their language is a Creole blend of European and African languages. Some Gullah words and phrases: *Time ober* (time passed quickly), *Keep ya tongue een ya teet* (keep your tongue in your teeth; shut your mouth; don't repeat what I just told you), *Lecket* (collect it), *Perenna* (marina), *Put fire een ya feet* (run real fast, hurry), *Frum de time de dew cum t dayclean* (from early evening until daylight the next morning), and *Mout mek yu backside lib high* (don't sass and keep gossip to yourself or somebody might give you a whipping). In the not-too-distant future, all trace of Gullah will have vanished from the low country as new generations dismiss the language, beliefs, and traditions of their forefathers. Every February the Native Islander Gullah Celebration takes place. It is a festival celebrating the food, music, art, and history of the Gullah culture. (800) 721-7120 and www.gullahcelebration.com.

❧ ❧ ❧

story attached. An enormous house used to sit on the highest bluff of Hilton Head Island. It was erected as the perfect home for a young man and his betrothed. After an elaborate wedding ceremony, the newlyweds and guests were transported to the island for a grand reception. The wedded pair were taken from the boat to the house. The bride beamed with delight when she saw her new home. She kissed her husband and whispered promises of devotion. As the couple was dancing, the groom noticed his bride was sweating profusely. Worried about her condition, he led her to a chair. Before they could reach it, she collapsed. Guests hurried to help, but the young man pushed them away and scooped up his trembling wife. Talking softly to her, he carried her into the house and up to their bedroom, while her long gown trailed the floor. A doctor was summoned, who confirmed what the frightened young man already suspected. His lovely bride had contracted the deadly fever, and nothing could be done for her. The husband sat by the bed all night, watching his love slowly die. By morning's light she had taken her last breath. His anguish was beyond anything he had believed he could feel. The most he could do for his betrothed was to build a spectacular mausoleum that would symbolize their love, and his loss, forever more.

It took many men and several days to build the monument as the young man had instructed. Finally, it was finished, and her body sealed inside. Every night from then on, the man visited the grave, sometimes

Sea Pines Plantation featuring Sound and Harbour Town Lighthouse.
Hilton Head Chamber of Commerce

sobbing violently, other times just sitting with his shoulders drooped and his head in his hands. He never got over her death and died within a few years, from a broken heart, many said. The enormous crypt was opened just long enough to place his coffin beside his wife's. After the Civil War, desperate looters dug up many graves, searching for heirlooms. Some tried to break into the mausoleum, but all met with horrible results. One grave robber was crushed by falling tile from the crypt's roof. One man gained entry, but was accidentally locked inside the vault when the heavy door swung shut behind him. His corpse was found by another marauder. It scared him so much when the bony figure fell out on him, the arms swinging around him as if embracing him, that he had a heart attack and never recovered. From then on, no one dared to disturb the crypt.

The mausoleum is the largest antebellum structure on the island and is in Zion Cemetery, which is at the intersection of Highway 278 and Matthew Road. $

The Coastal Discovery Museum is a nonprofit environmental and historical organization that hosts various tours including the Old House Plantation (a former rice plantation), Pinckney Island tour, schooner cruise, Ft. Mitchel tour with Civil War overview, beach tour, and more. There's also a continuously running historical video, numerous displays, and a gift shop. It is housed in the same facility as the Hilton Head Island Chamber of Commerce Welcome Center. 100 William Hilton Parkway. (843) 689-6767. Free.

Ft. Howell on Beach City Road was built in 1864 by Union troops to protect Mitchelville, a freedmen's village that existed for a short time after the Battle of Port Royal, Civil War. (800) 523-3373 or (843) 785-3673. $.

Ft. Mitchel at Hilton Head Plantation, circa 1862, was built to protect Hilton Head. (800) 523-3373 or (843) 785-3673. Free.

Harbour Town Marina and Lighthouse contains an observation tower at the top of the beacon that rewards climbers with a great view of the island and the Calibogue Sound. Plaques illustrating the history of Harbour Town and the lighthouse line the tower's interior. While it does serve as a navigational aid for boats coming into Harbour Town Marina, its main purpose is as a symbol of Sea Pines Plantation. The beacon is open daily. The marina has several gift shops and restaurants. A day pass can be purchased at the security gate of Sea Pines Plantation for those interested in visiting the marina. Ample parking is available. $

Hilton Head Lighthouse. This 95-foot beacon is one of only a handful of skeletal towers still in existence in America. It was built in 1880 of steel, wood, and cast iron. The lighthouse is located at the eighth hole of the Arthur Hills Golf Course at Palmetto Dunes Resort, open only to members and their guests. (843) 785-1161.

Nature & Wildlife

Pelicans, giant loggerhead turtles, bottlenose dolphins, bobcats, otters, minks, wild boar, alligators, and deer can be found. But don't hold your breath waiting for a bobcat or wild boar as they are shy and found only deep in the forest preserve and other remote, inaccessible spots on the island. Bird-watchers will delight in the 200 or more species of birds that flock to Hilton Head, including ospreys, snowy egrets, white ibis, cattle egrets, and great blue herons. For more information on nature and bird-watching walks (including hayrides, horseback tours, and a nighttime turtle watch walk), check with the Coastal Discovery Museum (843) 689-6767; Audubon-Newhall Preserve (843) 785-5775; Sea Pines Forest Preserve (843) 842-1449; and Sea Pines EcoTours (800) SEAPINES, (800) 732-7463, and (843) 363-4530.

The Town of Hilton Head is very protective of its island ecology and has published *The Green Guide*, which contains many important facts. It is illegal to feed dolphins in U.S. waters because they can get very sick from people food. Never walk on the sand dunes. Never tamper with a loggerhead turtle nest, even if you think you are being helpful. Visitors should call and request the guide or stop in and pick up a copy at the Hilton Head Island Chamber of Commerce.

Victoria Bluff Heritage Preserve is a 1,000-acre preserve that is perfect for hiking, fishing, horseback riding, and enjoying nature. The preserve is open year-round, and hunting is allowed seasonally. Wear bright-

❦ ❦ ❦

Hilton Head is popular with honeymooners and couples looking for a romantic getaway. In fact, couples often come to the island to get married or renew their vows—right on the beach. Contact A Wedding By The Sea. (843) 342-3981.

❦ ❦ ❦

ly colored clothing during hunting season. From Graves Bridge, which adjoins the island to the mainland, go west on US 278 for 2 miles. Turn right on Sawmill Creek Road and follow signs for the Waddell Mariculture Center. (843) 837-3795. Free.

ACTIVITIES

Adventure Cove is a family fun center. There's miniature golf, batting cages, a video arcade, bumper cars, a driving range, a motion theater and laser show, a roller coaster, a food court, and more. William Hilton Parkway and Folly Field Road at Mile Market 6, Hilton Head Island. (843) 842-9990 and www.adventurecove.com. $

Pirate's Island has two 18-hole miniature golf courses. (843) 686-4001 and www.hiltonheadisland.com/piratesisland. $

Main Street Lanes bowling alley is at 2600 Main Street. (843) 681-7750. $

HORSEBACK RIDING

Lawton Stables in Sea Pines provides horse rides through Sea Pines Forest Preserve. For novices, riding lessons are offered for an additional fee. Pony rides are available for youngsters. (843) 671-2586. $

Sea Horse Farms offers several daily beach rides. (843) 681-7746. $

BICYCLING

Thanks to safe and extensive public bike paths, bicycling is very popular on the island. All kinds of bikes and accompanying gear, for all ages, can be rented from these bike companies:

Island Cruisers, with free delivery and pick-up. (843) 785-4321.

Hilton Head Bicycle Company. (843) 686-6888.

Bikes Plus. (843) 671-5588.

Bicycle Club of Hilton Head, with free pick-up and delivery. (843) 842-BIKE and (843) 842-2453.

Pedals. (843) 842-5522.

Bikes, Kites & More. (843) 342-7530.

Hilton Head is a popular place to golf. Hilton Head Chamber of Commerce

G OLFING

Several tournaments take place on the island every year, including the MCI Classic-Heritage of Golf, Celebrity Golf Tournament, and *Golf World*/Palmetto Dunes Collegiate Invitational. According to the Hilton Head Chamber of Commerce, one million rounds of golf are played each year in Beaufort County generating more than $77 million annually. There are over twenty championship golf courses on Hilton Head and another twenty in close proximity, most of which are open to the public and resort guests.

Contact (888) GOLF-ISLAND, (888) 465-3475, and www.golfis-land.com to receive a free Hilton Head golf guide. There are some moderately-priced courses in nearby Bluffton, but most courses on Hilton Head, such as the George Fazio Course (named one of *Golf Digest*'s 100 top courses in US) and Shipyard Golf Club (a stop on the senior PGA tour), are expensive. When making your reservation, be sure to inquire about proper dress.

Golf schools offer hourly, daily, and weekly clinics:

Golf Academy of Hilton Head at Sea Pines. (800) 925-0467 and (843) 785-4540.

Golf Instruction at Hilton Head National. (843) 842-5900.

Golf Instruction by LPGA Professional Inez Long. (843) 757-GOLF.

Palmetto Dunes Golf Instruction Program, with women-only instruction. (843) 785-1138 and (800) 637-2694.

Palmetto Hall Golf Instruction Program. (843) 689-4100.

Hilton Head Island School of Golf. (843) 689-4100.

Indigo Run Golf Instruction Program. (843) 689-2200.

TENNIS

Tennis ranks right up there with golf on Hilton Head. There are 300 clay, grass, and hard courts on the island. Here's a list of the top-rated courts and tennis schools that offer lessons and clinics:

Hilton Head Island Beach & Tennis Resort. (843) 785-6613.
Palmetto Dunes Tennis Center. (843) 785-1152 and (800) 972-0257.
Port Royal Racquet Club. (843) 686-8803.
Sea Pines Racquet Club. (843) 363-4495 and (800) SEA-PINE.
Stan Smith Tennis Academy. (800) 845-6131 and (843) 363-4495.
US Professional Tennis Registry. (843) 785-7244.

WATER ACTIVITIES

There are dozens of companies that offer nature cruises, kayaking adventures, and fishing excursions. Here are some that are well-established. Additionally, there are nine public marinas on the island and all have many kinds of boats for rent.

Adventure Cruises features sightseeing cruises, a Daufuskie ferry, dinner cruises in the summer, deep sea fishing, dolphin-watching, and sunset cruises around Hilton Head, including Daufuskie Island. (843) 785-4558. $

Advanced Sail claims it offers "The Island's Most Fun Dolphin Watch Sailing Experiences." They also offer morning, afternoon, and sunset nature cruises. (843)-686-2582 and www.hiltonheadisland.com/sailing. $

Adventure Kayak Tours at Shelter Cove Marina offers canoe and kayak tours for exploration around Hilton Head Island and Pinckney Island Wildlife Refuge. (843) 816-5686. $

Island Water Sports at Hudson's Landing rents pontoon boats, fishing boats and equipment. The company also offers waterskiing, parasailing, dolphin-watch adventures, and kayak tours. (843) 689-6800. $

Cool Breeze Kayaking has bird-watching trips, guided nature tours (morning, sunset, and moonlight), and dolphin-watching. No experience necessary. Excursions, which leave from Pinckney Island Wildlife Refuge and Broad Creek, are led by experienced paddlers and naturalists. (877) 287-5154 and (843) 342-3699 and www.hiltonheadisland.com/kayak.htm. $

Southern Exposure Kayaking Adventures offers kayak eco-tours. All trips depart from Pinckney Island or Broad Creek. Choose from the fireworks display tour (summer), sunset, sunrise, or moonlight nature tours, ACE Basin, New River, Edisto River, or Colleton River outings. Kayak rentals are available. (843) 683-6900. $

Outside Hilton Head gives guided nature kayak tours including summer kids and teen kayak camps, clinics, lessons, and weekend retreats; dolphin nature tours; and full day kayak excursion. No experience is necessary. (800) 686-6996, (843) 686-6996, and www. outsidehiltonhead.com. $

Take a nature watching excursion aboard the sailing catamarans, **Flying Circus** or **Pau Hana**. Private charters are available. (843) 686-2582.

Water-Dog Outfitter provides kayak tours and rentals. No experience is necessary. (843) 683-2313. $

Enjoy a narrated environmental tour featuring dolphins and nature aboard the **S. S. Pelican**, a restored Navy motor whaler. Broad Creek Marina. (843) 681-2522 and www.hiltonheadisland.com/dolphin tour.htm $

Commander Zodiac at South Beach Marina rents sailboats and offers sailing lessons for all ages. They also have dolphin and nature watching tours and Daufuskie beachcombing aboard zodiac rafts. (843) 671-3344. $

H2O Sports Center at Sea Pines offers both instruction and rentals in kneeboarding, parasailing, waverunning, and hydrosliding. (843) 671-4FUN, (843) 671- 7007, and www.h2osportsonline.com. $

Island Scuba Dive & Travel provides scuba diving lessons, gear, and dive trips. (843) 689-3245. $

Island Water Sports offers waterskiing and waverunning. (843) 671-7007. $

Outside Hilton Head provides two-hour tours, daily guided kayak tours, and overnight camping trips to explore low-country coastal areas. (800) 686-6996, (843) 686-6996, and www.outsidehiltonhead.com. $

Spirit of Harbourtown offers sunset dinner cruises on the "island's only heated and air-conditioned luxury yacht." In the summer, they offer a sunset and fireworks dinner cruise one night a week and a family barbecue cruise one night a week. (843) 842-7179. $

F OR   THE   K IDS

Adventure Cruises at Shelter Cove Harbour provides daytime dolphin-watching or shark adventure cruises at night. (843) 785-4558. $

Drifter Excursions at South Beach Marina has a morning cruise where kids cast nets for shrimp and pull crab pots, or opt for a dolphin-watching expedition or family sunset cruise. (843) 363-2900. $

Waterfun Park on Tanglewood Drive has an arcade, waterslides, miniature golf, and more. (843) 842-8108. $

F ISHING

Hilton Head Island is a fisherman's paradise with sea trout, flounder, crokers, swordfish, shark, spot tail bass, bluefish, snapper, grouper, kingfish, cobia, and bluefish. A freshwater fishing license is required for anyone fishing the island's lakes or ponds September through December.

Saltwater fishing season runs April through October. No license required.

A Fishin' Mission offers fishing trips. (843) 785-9177.

Atlantic Fishing Charters at Harbour Town Yacht Basin provides day or night fishing. (843) 671-4534.

Bonanza Charters offers in-shore and offshore sports fishing charters. (843) 689-5873.

Captain Hook Deep Sea Fishing claims it has "the largest and most comfortable party fishing boat." (843) 785-4558 and (843) 683-9166.

Micabe offers offshore half-day, full day, and overnight sportfishing. The brochure says the *Micabe* is the fasting fishing boat on Hilton Head. (803) 785-3103 and (803) 842-7001.

Crabbing can best be accomplished near the docks and banks. *Crabber J. II* offers crabbing outings and dolphin-watching. (843) 785-4298.

ENTERTAINMENT & NIGHTLIFE

Blue Night Cafe has live music nightly. 4 Arrow Road. (843) 842-6683.

Coconuts Comedy Club at Heritage Square boasts top-notch comedians. (843) 686-6887.

Hilton Head Playhouse at Dunnagan's Alley/Arrow Road is a community playhouse that puts on first-rate musicals and plays. (843) 636-3945.

The Jazz Corner at Village at Wexford is a small jazz club that has top-name performers. (843) 842-8630.

Port Royal Clubhouse Dinner Theatre at Port Royal Plantation is a good place for those seeking dinner and a show. (843) 689-4653.

Monkey Business at Park Plaza is a sophisticated dance club that plays a wide array of music. (843) 686-3545.

The Lodge at Hilton Head Plaza is a cigar bar that offers billiards. (843) 842-8966.

Music enthusiasts might want to catch a performance by the **Hallelujah Singers,** which is Gullah culture storytelling through music. (843) 525-6129. $.

Hilton Head Orchestra performs October-May. (843) 842-2055. $.

Hilton Head Choral Society. (843) 681-8931. $.

The Self Family Arts Center at Shelter Cove offers a wide variety of arts exhibits and entertainment, such as Local Artists' Concert, Hallelujah Singers, Hilton Head Art League Show, and theater series. (843)-842-ARTS and www.artscenter-hhi.org. $.

ACCOMMODATIONS

Westin Resort, formerly the Hotel Inter-Continental at Port Royal

Plantation. (800) 937-8461, (843) 681-4000, and www.westin.com.

Crowne Plaza Resort Hilton Head Island. (800) 334-1881, (843) 842-2400, and www.crowneplazaresort.com.

Hyatt Regency Hilton Head Resort. (800) 233-1234, (843) 785-1234, and www.hyatthiltonhead.com.

Disney's Hilton Head Island Resort. (800) 341-2636, (843) 341-4081, and (843) 341-4000.

Marriott Vacation Club offers weekend value packages and "vacation ownership." (800) 845-5279.

If you're looking for someplace more subdued and tranquil than most beach resorts, you may want to try **Main Street Inn**. Located away from the beach, this upscale inn has loads of appeal, such as its thirty-four spacious rooms, European spa, lounges with fireplaces, pool, hot tub, afternoon tea, and more. (800) 471-3001 and www.mainstreetinn.com.

The **Inn at Harbour Town** is a sixty-room upscale hotel adjacent to the Harbour Town Clubhouse. (800) 732-7463 and (843) 363-8100 and www.seapines.com.

Comfort Inn & Suites. (800) 228-5150 and (843) 842-6662.

Fairfield Inn. (800) 228-2800, (843) 705-2300, and www.marriott.com/fairfieldinn.

Holiday Inn Oceanfront is great for families. Kids stay and eat free, and there is a Pizza Hut on the property, as well as a children's pool and playground, seasonal activities scheduled for kids, refrigerators and coffeemakers in the rooms, and many gift shops on site. (800) 423-9897 and (843) 785-5126.

VACATION RENTALS

Home rentals are a good deal for families because they have full kitchens that give the wallet a welcome rest at meal times and do not charge a per person rate. Choose from over 6,000 rental properties including houses, condos, and villas.

Adventure Inn & Villa Rentals offers oceanfront villas (one to three bedrooms) and homes with golf packages that include free use of the tennis courts and fitness club. There are children's programs during the summer. 41 South Forest Beach Drive, Hilton Head, SC 29938. (800) 845-9500, (843) 785-5151, and www.hhislandsc.com.

Barefoot Properties of Hilton Head has two- and three-bedroom villas for rent. 100 Courtyard Building, Hilton Head, SC 29928. (800) 232-8421 and www.barefootproperties.net.

Beach Properties of Hilton Head offers one- to four-bedroom oceanfront and beach-oriented houses and villas in Sea Pines, Palmetto Dunes, and mid-island. PO Box 3069, Hilton Head Island, SC 29928. (800) 671-5155 and www.beach-property.com.

Hilton Head Condo Hotline has weekly and monthly villa and house rentals, as well as golf packages at Forest Beach, Sea Pines, and Palmetto Dunes. (800) 258-5852 and (843) 785-2939.

Island Rentals & Real Estate offers numerous oceanfront and ocean-oriented homes and villas. Call for a free catalog. PO Box 5915, Hilton Head, SC 29938. (800) 845-6134 and www.irhhi.com.

Lancaster Resort Rentals also provides many different types of island accommodations. PO Box 7887, Hilton Head Island, SC 29938. (800) 845-7017 and www.lancasterrentals.com.

Shortline Vacation Home & Villa Rentals has over 300 rental properties with one to seven bedrooms. Call and request their free Vacation Guide detailing their selections. PO Box 6275, Hilton Head Island, SC 29938. (800) 334-5012 and www.shorelinerentals.com.

Hilton Head Central Reservations is probably the best source for all island accommodations, including hotels, condominiums, villas, and houses. This service also provides golf packages and pertinent island information. PO Box 5312, Hilton Head Island, SC 29938. (800) 845-7018.

Another resource is **(800) Hilton Head,** (800) 445-8664, and www.hiltonheadvacation.com.

CAMPGROUNDS

Stoney Crest Plantation. 419 May River Road, Highway 46, Bluffton. (843) 757-3249.

Outdoor Resorts. 43 Jenkins Road, Hilton Head. (800) 722-2365 and (843) 785-7699.

Outdoor Resorts Motor Coach. 133 Arrow Road, Hilton Head. (800) 845-9560 and (843) 681-3256.

RESTAURANTS

Hilton Head has over two hundred restaurants, cafés, and bistros featuring cuisine ranging from Thai to Italian. Whatever you prefer, be sure to sample Lowcountry cooking while visiting the island. Signature dishes, such as frogmore stew and she crab soup, shouldn't be missed. Local seafood includes shrimp, oysters, and blue crab. Be sure to check out the dining guide (in most hotel rooms on the island), ask your concierge for recommendations, or review the *Island Events* or *Where to Go on Hilton Head Island* or the *Official Dining Guide to Hilton Head Island* found at www.hiltonheadisland.com. Dinner reservations are highly recommended at most island restaurants.

Castaways is a raw bar on New Orleans Road that features many types of shellfish and fish—even alligator! (843) 686-2526.

Quarterdeck in Harbour Town is a waterfront eatery and bar that can be enjoyed by young adults and families alike. (843) 671-2222.

The Crazy Crab has a huge fresh fish menu and is very casual about dress and atmosphere but not about the food! Visit its Sea Pines Harbour Town or William Hilton Parkway locations. (843) 681-5021 and (843) 363-2722.

CQ's is in Harbour Town and features contemporary American cuisine with French influence. (843) 671-2779.

Old Oyster Factory Seafood & Steakhouse is built on the site of one of the island's original oyster canneries. The post-and-beam restaurant overlooks Broad Creek, Mile Marker 6. (843) 681-6040.

Old Fort Pub, in Hilton Head Plantation beside Ft. Mitchell, is a two level restaurant, surrounded by Spanish moss, that faces Skull Creek and the Intracoastal Waterway. (843) 681-2386.

Alexander's steaks and seafood. (843) 785-4999.

Antonio's Italian cuisine. (843) 842-5505.

Boathouse II serving Louisiana Cajun and Lowcountry seafood. (843) 681-3663.

Brian's American cuisine. (843) 681-6001.

Cafe at Wexford. (843) 686-5969),

The Captain's Table Continental cuisine. (843) 686-4300.

Charleston's Southern continental cuisine. (843) 785-5008.

La Normadie French cuisine. Jackets are suggested. (843) 785-7425.

La Maisonette French cuisine. Jackets are suggested. (843) 785-6000.

Fitzgerald's Continental cuisine. Local favorite. (843) 785-5151.

Scott's Fish Market serves local seafood, with indoor and outdoor dining and entertainment on the deck in the summer. (843) 785-7575.

Gaslight 2000 serves French cuisine and an extensive wine list. (843) 785-5814.

Charley's Crab Continental cuisine with an Asian influence. (843) 342-9066.

If you're looking for a good place to relax for a few minutes and recharge, you might want to stop in at **Planet Smoothie**. It claims to have "the best-tasting smoothies on the planet!" 11 Palmetto Bay Road, Hilton Head Island, SC 29928. (843) 842-9808 and www.planetsmoothie.com. Find a free printable "multi-purchase" coupon online.

Sweet Sensations is an old-fashioned ice cream parlor and sandwich shop. 1407 Main Street Village. (843) 689-6666.

Truffles at Sea Pines Plantation Continental and American cuisine. (843) 671-6136.

Recently, nearly one hundred local businesses joined up to offer a discount program called "Celebration." This is a great way to save money on activities and dining. There are two types of memberships: one-time visitor, which is a free, temporary membership, or a Diamond Club membership for frequent visitors and residents. For more information or to obtain a Visitor Packet, which contains two discount club cards, a brochure listing all participating businesses, and a newsletter, contact Celebration, PO Box 3211, Hilton Head Island, SC 29928. (843) 342-9190, info@celebrationusa.com, and www.celebrationusa.com.

SHOPPING

Hilton Head has many shopping possibilities, including the **Factory Outlets Shoppes on the Parkway**. 890 William Hilton Parkway (Highway 278) between Palmetto Dunes and Shipyard Plantation. (843) 686-6233.

ANNUAL EVENTS

Hilton Head is a great place to visit any time of the year. High season begins in March when several significant tennis and golf tournaments begin. Tourism slacks off during May, but kicks into high gear from June through August. Because of mild year-round temperatures and reduced rates, visiting off-season can be rewarding. Every year the Hilton Head Island Chamber of Commerce offers an Endless Summer promotion from mid-August to mid-November. (800) 523-3373.

Special summer activities include:

The nationally recognized **Fun for Kids! Program**. (843) 671-3590.

Shannon Tanner Children's Concerts. (843) 785-1106.

Gregg Russell Family Concerts. (843) 671-3590.

Summer events at **Coligny Plaza**. (843) 842-6050.

NEARBY POINTS OF INTEREST

Jenkins Island, located on Skull Creek at Port Royal Sound and adjacent to the Pinckney Island Wildlife Refuge, is a very small island that is home to the Outdoor Resorts Yacht Club.

Bluffton, located just a few minutes north of the island, began in 1825 as a summer retreat for plantation owners. Situated on the highest bluff on the May River, it is a historic village that offers a one-mile walking tour of several antebellum homes and structures. The best place to start is at the Heyward House Historic Center on Boundary Street. This former plantation home is a museum and headquarters for the Bluffton Historical Preservation Society. Walking tour maps may be obtained here. (843) 757-6293.

SAVANNAH

There are several tour companies that provide different day excursions to Savannah and its historic district.

Gray Line/Low Country Adventures. (912) 234-TOUR and (912) 234-8687.

Historic Bluffton's Church of the Cross, built in 1854. Terrance Zepke

Old Savannah Tours. (800) 517-9007.
Old Town Trolley Tours. (912) 233-0083.
Riverboat Cruises run year-round. River Street Riverboat Company, 9 East River Street. (800) 786-6404, (912) 232-6404, and www.savannah-riverboat.com.

The Savannah National Wildlife Refuge is 7,000 acres of flora and fauna. Off Highway 17, north of the Georgia border. (912) 652-4415.

Contact the **Savannah Area Convention & Visitor's Bureau** for more information. PO Box 1628, 222 West Oglethorpe Avenue, Suite 100, Savannah, GA 31402. (912) 944-0456.

TOURISM INFORMATION

The local newspaper is *The Island Packet,* and a good source of free tourist information is *Island Events.* The monthly magazine contains information on shopping, dining, entertainment, and more. Available at the Hilton Head Visitor Center and many area news stands. www.hilton-head.com/events.

Where to Go on Hilton Head is another free publication that is available at most news stands or visitors' centers. (843) 686-5808.

Hilton Head Island Chamber of Commerce Welcome Center. Visit the center for brochures on accommodations, restaurants, and activities, as well as to obtain a free, comprehensive map and directions to anywhere on the island. 100 William Hilton Parkway Hilton Head Island, SC 29926. (843) 689-6767.

Hilton Head Island Chamber of Commerce & Visitors Bureau.
One Chamber Drive Hilton Head Island, SC 29928. (800) 523-3373,
(843) 785-3673, and www.hiltonheadisland.org.

D I R E C T I O N S   &   A C C E S S I B I L I T Y
The island is open to the public and easily accessible. Take I-95 to
US 278, exit 8 to Hilton Head Island. Once you exit I-95, the drive is less
than thirty minutes. An intra-island toll road, the Cross Island Expressway,
was recently built to help traffic flow during peak seasons.

There is also an airport on the island, Hilton Head Airport. (843) 689-
5400, (843) 681-6386, and www.hiltonheadairport.com. There are also
airports in Savannah and Charleston.

ᵥ P I N C K N E Y   I S L A N D

Population: uninhabited

One of the first land grants for this island was issued to Alexander
Mackay in 1710. He sold it to a wealthy lawyer and judge, Charles
Pinckney, in 1734. Charles Pinckney, who lived in Charleston, bought the
island for his wife, Eliza. Her favorite hobby was botany, and the island
was a great place for her to study and experiment. The Pickneys left the
island to their son, Charles Cotesworth Pinckney, who served as a
Revolutionary War Commander, presidential candidate in 1804 and in
1808, and signer of the US Constitution. He and his wife built a manor
home on the island in 1801. The beautiful house was destroyed during a
hurricane. In the 1900s, James Bruce bought the island as a hunting
retreat.

The island now serves as a refuge for wading birds, shorebirds, waterfowl, and other animals. According to refuge management, the osprey and
ibis ponds are the most accessible and provide the best wildlife viewing,

Pinckney Island is a nature lover's paradise, but beware of the overgrowth. Terrance Zepke

including turtles, snakes, frogs, egrets, herons, ducks, wood storks, otters, deer, sandpipers, oystercatchers, and more. Pinckney Island National Wildlife Refuge is on Calibogue Sound and contains 4,052 acres of salt marsh and small islands. Fourteen miles of trails run through the refuge and visitors are permitted to explore on foot or on bicycle.

According to literature found at the refuge's information station, "All trips begin and end at the parking area located half a mile from the refuge entrance." No cars are permitted beyond the parking lot. I found a good-sized trail but it only circled back. I visited the refuge at the end of summer and overgrowth may have diminished the trails. The map supplied at the information station indicates the first stop is the ibis pond, approximately one mile from the refuge entrance. Since there was no navigable trail, I never made it to this pond or any other place listed on the map.

Saltwater fishing and shellfishing, by boat only, are permitted. There is a public boat ramp for Skull Creek and Intracoastal Waterway at Last End Point. There are no amenities on the island, and pets are not allowed. As in any wildlife refuge, watch for snakes and alligators. Do not feed or disturb the alligators. Insect repellent is highly recommended. Summer is probably not the best time to visit because of insects and the intense humidity. Permits are required for hunting. Questions regarding hunting or any refuge activities should be directed to the Savannah Coastal Refuges Office, Parkway Business Center, Suite 10, 1000 Business Center Drive, Savannah, GA 31405. (912) 652-4415.

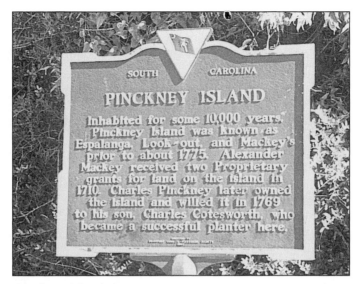

Pinckney Island sign. Terrance Zepke

ACTIVITIES

Cool Breeze Kayaking has bird-watching trips, guided nature tours (morning, sunset, and moonlight), and dolphin-watching. No experience is necessary. Excursions, which leave from Pinckney Island Wildlife Refuge and Broad Creek, are led by experienced paddlers and naturalists. (877) 287-5154, (843) 342-3699, and www. hiltonheadisland.com/kayak.htm. $

Southern Exposure Kayaking Adventures offers kayak eco-tours. All trips depart from Pinckney Island or Broad Creek. Choose from the fireworks display tour in the summer; sunset, sunrise, or moonlight nature tours; ACE Basin, New River, Edisto River, or Colleton River outings. Kayak rentals are available. (843) 683-6900. $

Pinckney Island Kayak Company offers guided tours through the refuge. Tours led by experienced paddlers and naturalists. No experience is necessary. (843) 342-3159. $

NEARBY POINTS OF INTEREST

Savannah National Wildlife Refuge is at the southernmost point of the state, and more than three hundred species of birds make their way here seasonally. (912) 652-4415.

TOURISM INFORMATION

Hilton Head Island Chamber of Commerce & Visitors Bureau. One Chamber Drive, Hilton Head Island, SC 29928. (800) 523-3373, (843) 785-3673, and www.hiltonheadisland.org.

BEAUFORT ISLANDS

DIRECTIONS & ACCESSIBILITY
Admission is free and visitors are allowed daily during daylight hours. Take US 278 past Graves Bridge, a half of a mile west of Hilton Head Island.

☙ DAUFUSKIE ISLAND

Population: 200

This five-mile-long and two-and-one-half-mile-wide sea island is bordered on the north by the Cooper River, by Mungen River on the southern side, New River on the west, and Calibogue Sound and the Atlantic Ocean on the east. It is one nautical mile from Hilton Head Island and is South Carolina's southernmost sea island. The Indian word, Daufuskie, roughly translates to land with a point. This land is believed to be 80,000 to 120,000 years old, and has been inhabited almost continuously for 4,000 years.

In 1664, Yemasee Indians came to Daufuskie. Before that, the Cusabo Indians lived on the island. Robert Sanford, newly appointed Clerk and Register for the Lords Proprietors of the new Carolina county (it wasn't called South Carolina until 1693), used Indian guides to explore Daufuskie and area islands in 1666. It has been spelled many ways over the years, starting with the earliest land grant for 500 acres on "Dawffus Tee Island" to Thomas Cowte on November 15, 1707.

During the Revolutionary War, Daufuskie was often referred to as Little Bermuda because, like Bermuda, it served as a Tory refuge. A fortification was built here by the Royal Militia in 1781. Revolutionary War Whigs of Hilton Head attacked property on Daufuskie in 1781, as retribution for an assault by the Daufuskie Tory Loyalists on Hilton Head.

From about 1862 to 1867, four young, white school teachers, sent by the American Missionary Association, taught on Daufuskie Island. Two

One of the Island's historic landmarks is the Mary Fields Elementary School, which is now used as a medical clinic. Terrance Zepke

lived in Melrose Mansion and two resided at Lawton Plantation. Classes lasted three hours each day and there was also a night session for older children or adults who had to work during the day. The four women schooled ninety black students. In 1911, another teacher, Sarah Constable, arrived on Daufuskie to teach the white children. She lived at Melrose until the mansion burned down the following year.

That same year, the island got its first official postmaster, Evelyn Stoddard, who received no salary, just commission on the few stamps she sold. The post office had previously been the tack room of an old barn. Mrs. Billie K. Burn, author of a wonderful book, *An Island Named Daufuskie*, was the island's seventh postmaster and served from 1963 to 1984.

There were eleven plantations on the island when the Civil War broke out. Practically all of Daufuskie was farmed in the late 1800s and early 1900s. The early 1900s was the height of economic good times, thanks to Sea Island cotton, indigo, lumber, and oysters. Planters grew pecans, pears, figs, tomatoes, and other produce and exported it through Savannah, Bluffton, Beaufort, and Charleston. Some days, as many as five steamships were loaded at the dock or anchored offshore waiting to be loaded. In 1920, the boll weevil ended the prosperous cotton production, but oysters still brought a good living to residents.

Oystering is the only continuous industry the island has ever known. A cannery, L. P. Maggioni Company, was on the island until 1903. An oys-

This Daufuskie Island church is still used for weekly services. It is also one of the island's historical structures. Terrance Zepke

ter-shucking factory was on Daufuskie until the late 1930s. Oystering was a way of life from the 1880s to 1959, when polluted waters ruined oyster beds. The Great Depression forced many islanders to go elsewhere for work. Only three hundred residents remained to work in the oyster canneries. During the Depression, men that weren't employed by WPA or CCC, made a living in creative ways, including operating moonshine stills, becoming trappers of otters, minks, possums, and raccoons. These furs brought good money at Savannah furriers.

During World War II, the US Coast Guard set up a station at Melrose. They patrolled the beach on horses accompanied by dogs and ran phone wires along the entire beach so they could communicate with headquarters at Melrose Base. In 1943, three Germans arrived at the island in a submarine. They stole a rowboat, but got caught on the mainland. Another time, patrols spotted a sub and notified Melrose Base, which in turn contacted Hilton Head. Within thirty minutes, planes from Hunter Field in Savannah dropped four bombs where the last sighting had been. Later, some articles of clothing, life jackets, and a few oil slicks washed ashore. It is believed the sub was sunk during the bombing.

Many families left the island during World War II to work in a Savannah shipyard, so population greatly diminished and the Daufuskie School closed. In 1953, everyone on the island had electricity, but it wasn't until 1973 that telephone service reached Daufuskie. The Daufuskie School shut down permanently in 1962. The first white teacher at Mary Fields

View of the Daufuskie Island resort main inn and gazebo. Terrance Zepke

Elementary on Daufuskie was Pat Conroy, who began teaching in 1969. The principal taught grades 1–4 and Conroy instructed grades 5–8. Pat Conroy was both the first white teacher and first male teacher in the school's history. He later became a successful author and his first novel, *The Water Is Wide,* is based on his experiences as a teacher on Daufuskie. It was published in 1972 and was later made into the motion picture "Conrack." He became an author after he was fired by the Beaufort County School Board for an unauthorized leave of absence; Conroy accepted a consulting job with University of South Carolina in order to

The resort's golf course and beach. Terrance Zepke

❧ ❧ ❧

Daufuskie plantations were two hundred to 1,100 acres. Almost everything needed was grown or raised on a plantation so as to be self-sufficient. Exceptions included sugar and clothing. Herbs for seasoning and plants used to make poultices for the sick were grown. Fruits and vegetables were produced year-round. Tallow (used for making candles and soap) came from the fat of the cow and cooking lard came from the fat of the pig. Meats were cured or smoked. Cow hides were used to make harnesses, shoes, and other leather goods. Cows and goats supplied milk, butter, and cheese. Bees were kept for making honey. Two kinds of soap were made, both soft and hard. Soft was for scrubbing floors and washing dishes. Hard soap was used for bathing and washing clothes.

The *Massa* (planter) handled finances, slaves, and supervised the plantations. He made all executive decisions. His wife was the *Missus*, and her role was to take care of her children, plan the daily menu, make sure the slaves had what they needed, and supervise the making of medicinal poultices. While the planter was away, his next in command, a white *Overseer* (supervisor), assumed his duties and looked after the planter's family. The *Driver* was a slave who had some authority and reported directly to the overseer. He assigned tasks and made sure the slaves performed them.

❧ ❧ ❧

---

finance a school field trip to Six Flags Amusement Park. He sued for reinstatement but lost the case.

Haig's Point, on the north end of the island, was purchased by International Paper Corporation in 1984 for nearly $8.5 million, with an option to buy additional land. They renamed it Haig Point and hired a restoration specialist to oversee renovations to the Haig Point Lightkeeper's House. During the work, they discovered the foundation of the largest tabby structure found on the state's sea islands. A glass plate was installed in the floor to showcase the tabby foundation. This land was eventually developed into Haig Point Club, an upscale residential community.

Daufuskie Properties developed Melrose in 1987. Overlooking Calibogue Sound and the Atlantic Ocean, Melrose Club is a 663-acre residential community. Bloody Point Club is a 340-acre residential community established on the southern end of the island in 1991. Bloody Point got its name because of two Indian massacres that happened during the Yemasee War of 1715. In 1997, Melrose Club and Bloody Point Club

The Silver Dew Pottery. Terrance Zepke

merged as part of an acquisition by ClubCorp, Inc., to become the Daufuskie Island Resort. Both communities have championship golf courses, swimming and tennis, and residents are allowed to join the Daufuskie Island Club & Resort.

There are no accommodations, restaurants, or entertainment on the island besides what the resort offers. Daufuskie is an eclectic mix of old island life and changing times. Part of the island looks much as it did many years ago, but where development has taken place, with the residential communities and private resorts, things are very different. Like most of the state's islands, Daufuskie is struggling to preserve its heritage and still embrace changing times. Long-time Daufuskie inhabitants refer to past events as B. D. or A.D., meaning before development or after development. Tourism has revitalized the island. Daufuskie Island was accepted onto the National Register of Historic Places in 1982.

TOURS & ATTRACTIONS

The **Silver Dew Pottery** is a worthwhile stop just to hear about owner Bob Burn's experiences. He has sailed across the Atlantic in an old sailboat three times! And he knows the island history and will share it with visitors, as well as patiently answer questions about anything and everything. His grandfather, Pappy Burn, came to Daufuskie in 1898. He was a lighthouse keeper for the Bloody Point Lighthouse and operated a winery on the island in the 1950s. Bob's mother is Billie Burn, author of *An Island Named Daufuskie*. According to Bob and his wife, Emily, special pieces

Bob Burn at the Silver Dew Pottery. Terrance Zepke

of pottery are made with raised buttons, beads, and incisions to reflect the Indian pottery they have found on the island. The pottery is displayed in a workshop located in front of the Burns residence. The Burns will provide transportation from the Daufuskie dock to Silver Dew Pottery with advance arrangements. 18 Benjie's Point Road. (843) 842-6419. Free

The Daufuskie Island Resort offers a **Daufuskie Island History Tour** for resort guests. It includes island highlights: Daufuskie Island Elementary School, Janie Hamilton School, Mt. Carmel Baptist Church No. 2, First Union African Baptist Church (1884), Mary Fields School (where Pat Conroy taught from 1969 to 1970), Bloody Point Beach, Mary Dunn Cemetery (1790), and Silver Dew Pottery.

ACTIVITIES

Commander Zodiac at South Beach Marina rents sailboats and offers sailing lessons for all ages. They also offer Daufuskie beachcombing aboard zodiac rafts. (843) 671-3344. $

Adventure Cruises features sightseeing cruises, a Daufuskie ferry, dinner cruises in the summer, deep sea fishing, dolphin-watching, and sunset cruises around Hilton Head, including Daufuskie Island. (843) 785-4558. $

Hilton Head's Shelter Cove offers **Gullah Heritage Daufuskie Island Cruise and Land Tours**. This combines a narrated sightseeing cruise with two hours on Daufuskie Island when passengers may opt to take a guided bus tour of historic points of interest, rent golf carts or bicycles, or simply relax on the beach. Two-hour sunset dinner cruises are also available.

December 23, 1989, marked the first time in recorded history that it
snowed on Daufuskie for Christmas.

The renowned Daufuskie Deviled Crab recipe was first prepared in
1920. Mrs. Kizsie Bryan created it for a party and everyone
loved the deviled crab so much that she started selling them at
church picnics and for boat excursions. The tasty snacks sold
for fifteen cents each.

In 1878, the toll was fifty cents for a round-trip ferry ride
from Daufuskie to Savannah aboard *City of Bridgeton*.

Over the years, there have been three Secret Orders on Daufuskie
Island: The Oyster Union Society (established in 1919), The Knights of
Pythias (established in 1916), and The Odd Fellows (established in
1927). The Knights of Pythias and The Odd Fellows were men-only
groups that required initiations testing a potential member's bravery.

---

(843) 785-4558. $

The Beach Club offers three pools, a Jacuzzi, a fitness center, basket-ball and volleyball, cabana and chairs, and organized water sports (fishing, sailing, kayaking, parasailing, water skiing, and wave runners) for resort guests. (843) 842-2000. $

The **Equestrian Center** offers several options for resort guests, including the lesson trail, the Melrose trail, and the beach walk-trot. There are also clinics for riders of all ages and levels. (843) 842-2000. $

Lessons and clinics are offered for golf and tennis. Resort guests may play Daufuskie's golf courses and there is a miniature golf course the whole family can enjoy. Daufuskie Island Resort offers day golf packages for those interested in just coming over for the day. Golfers are transported on the resort's private passenger ferry. (843) 842-2000 and www.daufuskieresort.com.

ACCOMMODATIONS

Daufuskie Island Club & Resort is part of Pinehurst Company Resorts, owned and operated by ClubCorp. Guests may choose to stay in the Melrose Inn, an antebellum style inn with fifty-two rooms, or in two- or four-bedroom cottages that include a living and dining room, a full kitchen, a washer and dryer, and a porch with marsh or ocean view. Pets are not allowed. There are four restaurants and lounges, ranging from casual to fine dining. Recreational programs are offered during the summer and the holidays for kids and teenagers. Baby-sitting services are also available. There are ample conference and meeting facilities, including state-of-the-art audio-visual equipment. Charcoal grills and video rentals, groceries, gift items, and alcoholic beverages may be acquired at The General Store. The resort also has a deli that sells rotisserie chicken and sandwiches. Supplies may also be purchased at the Embarkation Center Island Shop. (843) 842-2000 and www.daufuskieresort.com.

NEARBY POINTS OF INTEREST

Turtle Island is in Jasper County, South Carolina, between Daufuskie Island and Savannah. It is 1,700 acres of marsh, maritime forest, and beach. Hunting is permitted according to state regulations. Visitation must be pre-arranged by making an appointment. Accessible by boat only. (843) 726-8126.

Tours of historic Savannah are offered by several companies:

Old Savannah Tours. (800) 517-9007.

Old Town Trolley Tours. (912) 233-0083.

River Street Riverboat Company with murder afloat cruises, Sunday brunch cruises, moonlight entertainment cruises, holiday theme cruises, and narrated sightseeing cruises. (800) 786-6404.

Gray Line Tours. (912) 234-8687.

Savannah Area Convention & Visitors Bureau. PO Box 1628, 222 West Oglethorpe Avenue, Suite 100, Savannah GA, 31402-1628. (877) 728-2662, (912) 944-0455, and www.savannahvisit.com.

TOURISM INFORMATION

Hilton Head Island Chamber of Commerce & Visitors Bureau. One Chamber Drive, Hilton Head Island, SC 29928. (800) 523-3373, (843) 785-3673, and www.hiltonheadisland.org.

Daufuskie Island Resort. PO Box 23285, Hilton Head Island, SC 29925. (800) 648-6778, (843) 842-2000, and www.daufuskieresort.com.

DIRECTIONS & ACCESSIBILITY

The island is accessible by boat only. **Calibogue Cruises** takes passengers from Hilton Head to Daufuskie Island and Savannah by appointment. 1 Freeport Lane, Daufuskie Island. (843) 342-8687.

Haig Point, a members-only residential development, runs a ferry for its members. The county boat transports island school kids and interested tourists. The free shuttle departs early morning and early afternoon. Private.

Daufuskie Island Resort runs a ferry for its guests and those who have purchased golf packages. It departs Hilton Head early in the morning and late at night. $

There are daily water taxis that take Daufuskie Island Resort guests on the ten-minute journey to Hilton Head's Harbour Town.

Only resort guests and members are admitted at Haig Point or Daufuskie Resort. There is no public transport on the island. In season, day tours can be accomplished through Shelter Cove on Hilton Head. Additionally, golf carts and bicycles can be rented at the Daufuskie dock. However, if you are not familiar with the island, it is difficult to find some of its points of interest.

ADDITIONAL
RESOURCES

ORGANIZATIONS

❧ **South Carolina Department of Parks, Recreation, & Tourism.** Free highway maps and comprehensive vacation guides are available through this office. 1205 Pendleton Street, Suite 106, Columbia, SC 29201. (888) 88-PARKS, (803) 734-0122, www.discoversouthcarolina.com, www.south-carolinaparks.com, generalinfo@scprt.com, travelinfo@scprt.com, and parksinfo@scprt.com.

❧ **South Carolina State Chamber of Commerce.** 1201 Main Street, Suite 1810, Columbia, SC 29201. (800) 799-4601, (803) 799-4601, and www.sccc.org.

❧ **National Park Service.** Southeast Region, 100 Alabama Street SW, 1924 Building Atlanta, GA 30303. (404) 562-3100 and www.nps.gov.

❧ **US Fish & Wildlife Service.** (800) 344-WILD and www.fws.gov.

❧ **Low Country Tourism Office.** PO Box 615, Yemassee, SC 29945. (800) 528-6870, (843) 717-3090, come2sc@hargray.com, and www.lowcountrytravel.org.

❧ *The Low Country Companion* is "a guide to art, nature, history, ecotourism, dining, shops, accommodations, and golf in Georgetown, Pawley's Island, Litchfield Beach, Murrells Inlet, and Conway, South Carolina." Available through subscription or free at most low country visitors' centers. PO Box 2098, Pawley's Island, SC 29686. (843) 237-3899.

BOOKS

During my research on this book, I relied on many sources, including local and state tourism offices, local and state Chambers of Commerce, the South Carolina State Archives, the Library of Congress, local residents, island developers, and non-profit or state government agencies. Additionally, there are some excellent books that document island histo-

191

ry, folklore, nature, and wildlife that were extremely helpful.

Beaufort and the Sea Islands. Federal Writers Guide Project, 1938.

Burn, Billie. *An Island Named Daufuskie.* The Reprint Company, 1991.

Campani, Catherine Messmer and Halcomb, C. Andrew. *South Carolina's Low Country-A Past Preserved.* Sandlapper Publishing, 1988.

Puckette, Clara Childs. *Edisto: A Sea Island Principality.* Seaforth Publications, 1978.

Cole, Nathan. *The Road to Hunting Island South Carolina.* Arcadia Publishing, 1997.

Dabbs, Edith M. *Sea Island Diary: A History of St. Helena Island.* The Reprint Company, 1983.

Gleasoner, Diana and Bill. *Sea Islands of the South.* The East Woods Press, 1980.

Jerman, Patricia L. *South Carolina Nature Viewing Guide.* South Carolina Department of Natural Resources, 1998.

Jordan, Laylon Wayne. *A Place called St. John's Island: The Story of John's, Edisto, Wadmalaw, Edisto, Kiawah, and Seabrook.* The Reprint Company, 1998.

Marion, John Francis. *The Charleston Story.* Stackpole Books, 1978.

Menedez, Al and Shirley. *South Carolina Trivia.* Rutledge Hill Press, 1996.

Meyer, Peter. *Nature Guide to the Carolina Coast.* Avian-Cetacean Press, 1991.

Mitchell, Allen. *Wadmalaw Island.* Boar Hog Tree Press, 1996.

Graydon, Nell S. *Tales of Edisto.* The R. L. Bryan Company, 1955.

Parsons, Elsie. *Folklore of the Sea Islands.* Afro-Am Press, 1969.

Prevost, Charlotte Kaminski and Wilder, Effie Leland. *Pawley's Island . . . A Living Legend.* The State Printing Company, 1972.

Rhyne, Nancy. *Chronicles of the South Carolina Sea Islands.* John F. Blair Publishing, 1998.

Rogers, George C. *The History of Georgetown County, South Carolina.* University of South Carolina Press, 1970.

QUIZ

If you feel like testing your knowledge about places discussed in this book, take this short quiz.

1. What is the state seashell?
2. What is the state fish?
3. What is the oldest fishing village in South Carolina?
4. What year was Charles Towne renamed Charleston?
5. Where is the only tea plantation in America?
6. What tiny island is home to 150 people? Hint: It's surrounded by the Waccamaw and Pee Dee Rivers.
7. Isle of Palms was originally called what?
8. What town is South Carolina's second oldest town? Hint: It was founded in 1711.
9. What is the southernmost island off the South Carolina coast?
10. Where did the Marquis de Lafayette land when he arrived to join the American Revolutionary forces?
11. Old Point is the National Historic District of what town?
12. Which town calls itself the "Ghost Capital of the World?"
13. Where did President Abraham Lincoln establish a cemetery in 1863? *Hint: Nine thousand Union soldiers are buried here.*
14. Where did the US Marine Corps send a detachment during World War II because they were expecting an attack by the Germans?
15. Murrells Inlet is home to what famous writer? Hint: He wrote mystery and detective stories.
16. What character from *Gone With the Wind* was "reared in Charleston"?
17. Marsh Island is a rookery for what bird?
18. Over 280 species of birds have been sighted in what 250,000-acre forest?
19. Where was a nudist colony briefly established during the 1930s?
20. Closest to what island is the best surf fishing for sea trout, bluefish, whiting, flounder, and channel bass?
21. What rare plant can be found nowhere else in the state but Horry County?
22. What is the longest black water river in the world? Hint: It stretches for over 200 miles.
23. Why do many buildings in Charleston have metal plates in the walls?
24. In what year did a Great Flood occur in South Carolina?
25. What is the lowest temperature ever recorded in South Carolina?

26. What hurricane savagely attacked South Carolina coast in 1989?
27. What is the state bird?
28. What disease killed more than 7,400 South Carolina citizens in 1918?
29. The largest sawmill in the world in the 19th century was in what county?
30. What is a marsh tackey?

ANSWERS

1. Lettered olive
2. Striped bass
3. Murrells Inlet
4. 1783
5. Wadmalaw Island
6. Sandy Island
7. Long Island
8. Beaufort
9. Daufuskie Island
10. North Island
11. Beaufort
12. Georgetown
13. National Cemetery in Beaufort
14. Hilton Head Lighthouse
15. Mickey Spillane
16. Rhett Butler
17. Brown pelican
18. Francis Marion National Forest
19. Cat Island
20. Capers Island
21. Venus fly-trap
22. Edisto River
23. Instead of rebuilding after the Great Earthquake of 1886,
24. 1916
25. 19° F at Caesers Head on January 21, 1985
26. Hugo
27. Carolina Wren
28. Spanish influenza
29. Georgetown
30. A wild pony that used to roam Edingsville, an island off Edisto Island

citizens used bolts and turnbuckles to put buildings back together

I N D E X

Page numbers in **bold** refer to photographs. Due to space limitation, most hotels, shops, restaurants, and festivals are not included in the index. These listings can be found itemized in each book section.

If you enjoyed reading this book, here are some other Pineapple Press titles you might enjoy as well. To request our complete catalog or to place an order, write to Pineapple Press, P.O. Box 3889, Sarasota, Florida 34230, or call 1-800-PINEAPL (746-3275). Or visit our website at www.pineapplepress.com.

The Best Ghost Tales of North Carolina by Terrance Zepke. The actors of North Carolina's past linger among the living in this thrilling collection of ghost tales. Experience the chilling encounters told by the winners of the North Carolina "Ghost Watch" contest. Use Zepke's tips to conduct your own ghost hunt. ISBN 1-56164-233-9 (pb)

Ghosts of the Carolina Coasts by Terrance Zepke. Taken from real-life occurrences and Carolina Lowcountry lore, these 32 spine-tingling ghost stories take place in prominent historic structures of the region. ISBN 1-56164-175-8 (pb)

Bansemer's Book of Carolina and Georgia Lighthouses by Roger Bansemer. Written and illustrated in the same engaging style as Bansemer's Florida book, this volume accurately portrays how each lighthouse along the coasts of the Carolinas and Georgia looks today. ISBN 1-56164-194-4 (hb)

Lighthouses of the Carolinas by Terrance Zepke. Eighteen lighthouses aid mariners traveling the coasts of North and South Carolina. Here is the story of each, from origin to current status, along with visiting information and photographs. Newly revised to Include up-to-date information on the long-awaited and much-debated Cape Hatteras Lighthouse move, plus websites for area visitors' centers and tourist bureaus. ISBN 1-56164-148-0 (pb)

Pirates of the Carolinas by Terrance Zepke. Thirteen of the most fascinating buccaneers in the history of piracy, including Henry Avery, Blackbeard, Anne Bonny, Captain Kidd, Calico Jack, and Stede Bonnet. ISBN 1-56164205-3 (pb)

Guide to the Gardens of South Carolina by Lilly Pinkas. Organized by region, this guide provides detailed information about the featured species and facilities offered by South Carolina's public gardens. Includes 8 pages of color photos and 40 line drawings. ISBN 1-56164-251-7 (pb)